THE

DIDI MAN:
MY LOVE AFFAIR WITH
LIVERPOOL

THE DIDI MAN: MY LOVE AFFAIR WITH LIVERPOOL

DIETMAR HAMANN

with
Malcolm McClean

headline

First published in 2012
by HEADLINE PUBLISHING GROUP

2

Cataloguing in Publication Data is available from the British Library

Hardback ISBN 978 0 7553 6280 6
Trade paperback ISBN 978 0 7553 6383 4

Something: Words and music by George Harrison © 1969

Typeset in Cronos Pro by Palimpsest Book Production Limited, Falkirk, Stirlingshire

Printed and bound in Great Britain by
Clays Ltd, St Ives plc

Headline's policy is to use papers that are natural, renewable and recyclable products and
made from wood grown in sustainable forests. The logging and manufacturing processes
are expected to conform to the environmental regulations of the country of origin.

HEADLINE PUBLISHING GROUP
An Hachette UK Company
338 Euston Road
London NW1 3BH

www.headline.co.uk
www.hachette.co.uk

CONTENTS

FOREWORD BY JOHN BISHOP

Whenever I have read a foreword in someone's book it's always clear to me that it has been written by a friend of the author. It's always full of praise for the author's endeavours that have led to the publication of the book in order to whet the reader's appetite for what is to come. I am not going to do that for two reasons. One, I am not Didi Hamann's friend; and two, I spent years watching Didi play and if the foreword of a book is like the literary equivalent of a prematch warm-up, I have decided to act as Didi did in every game I saw him warm up for, by putting in no effort whatsoever.

Every Liverpool supporter will recall the feeling of anticipation before the game – taking your seat, talking about possible formations, tactics, game plans and scenarios that we might see in the course of the next ninety minutes. Then looking at the players warming up in the same way you would look at racehorses before a race, trying to see the telltale signs of who was best prepared for what was to come. Then you would see Didi Hamann looking like someone in a shoe shop with his wife. His face seeming to suggest that he knew he had to be there but he would rather be in the pub or on the couch with a cup of tea.

Other players would be bending and stretching, pulling this way and that so that the muscles in their finely tuned bodies were ready to burst into action. I've only ever seen Didi touch his toes once and that was when we played Fulham in the 2003/04 season when he bent over to tie his bootlaces.

The reality was that Didi came alive when the whistle blew and he had the ability to make something brilliant look easy. It always seemed to be that the bigger the game the more he took it in his stride and he would often leave the field looking like he had in fact wandered around a shoe shop rather than playing at the highest level of the greatest game in the world. All that Didi needed to do was to convert his World Cup runners-up medal to a winners' medal, pick up a EURO and a Premier League title and he would have then won every single trophy you can win in Germany, England and the world. Three medals away from a full set for a man who looked like he drove a van to work.

I think I need to clarify my earlier comment about Didi not being my friend. I do like the man, I like him a lot, and I have been lucky enough to spend time with him socially. Anyone who has done so will tell you that it is so enjoyable that you find yourself thinking that every stereotype you have about Germans is wrong. He is not in the least bit efficient, I have never met anyone who forgets what he is meant to be doing so often. He is a million miles from being stylish, and often looks like an eight-year-old who insists on dressing himself even though nothing matches. He's funny too. Very, very funny. Perhaps the reason he has stayed so long in England is that he simply does not belong in Germany any more. How many inefficient, badly dressed, funny Germans do you know?

No. The reason I said he is not my friend is because you do not keep secrets from friends (unless you are John Terry but that is another story), but I have always kept a secret from Didi, and that is that he changed my life and I owe much of what I am today to him. Not just him obviously, there have been loads of people who have influenced my life, but I am a comedian today due in no small part to the events of 25 May 2005.

In 2005, as Liverpool were progressing through the Champions League and stand-up comedy was just a sideline for me, I had a proper job. One day I was called into my boss's office and was told that my job depended upon me attending a meeting on 25 May. This was the same day that the final was to be played in Istanbul. The problem was that the meeting was to be in Seattle on the west coast of America, and it was physically impossible to be in both places at once.

Even after the momentous semi-final win against Chelsea, when I danced on the Kop and celebrated with my mates, I knew that I could not go to the final. It had been made clear to me that if I did not go to Seattle I would not have a job, so I reluctantly gave my ticket to one of my mates and boarded the plane for America.

Once in the States it became apparent that the meeting was not such a big deal and though I could not get to Istanbul, provided I caught all the right connections I could get home to watch the match in my own house.

Nineteen hours later I came through the door with ten minutes to spare before kick-off. All of my mates who had gone to Istanbul had sent their wives and kids to our house. I was the only man in the room. Little girls were all doing cartwheels in front of the telly. I'm thinking, 'What the hell am I doing here? I should be in Istanbul.'

At half-time we were 3–0 down and were being battered. Like every fan who had not made it to Istanbul I was filled with the mixed emotions of sadness and relief. It was like finding out that your wife has had sex with your best mate and she's told you that he was rubbish and only had a little willy.

Half-time and Didi came on and took control. Fifteen minutes later it was 3–3 and there was a chance that this would be the greatest comeback of all time.

And then it hit me. I should be in Istanbul. The only reason I was sitting here on the couch was purely because I had a job and somebody else was telling me what to do. Then Didi, with a broken bone in his foot, scored the first penalty in the shoot-out and took us on to win the Champions League.

That was like finding out that your wife had sex with your best mate, told you he was rubbish, he had a small willy and then seeing him get run over by a bus. I was sad, relieved and then deliriously happy.

But I wasn't there. I was sitting in the living room jet-lagged, listening to my mates phoning me up from Istanbul to say what an amazing night they were having. At that moment I decided that I would never ever again be told what to do for the sake of a job.

One week later I handed in my notice and said, 'That's it. Come hell or high water I am going to try and make it as a comedian. Then I'll be able to go to any final I want to.'

Didi had a direct effect on me doing the job that I'm doing now. How strange it's worked out. I'm doing OK. If it hadn't worked out that way I would have been knocking on Didi's door asking him to pay my mortgage.

He wasn't the only one who played a part in that momentous night. But every football supporter knows that when Didi came on to the pitch he took control and did the things that we knew he could do. Things that changed the game.

For my money he won us the Champions League. That will always be remembered and that's why he will always have such a special relationship with Liverpool supporters.

Prior to Didi coming to Liverpool the only thing that Scousers and Germans had in common was their propensity to grow dodgy moustaches and adopt weird hairstyles. But Didi is a cultural ambassador. He is the only German Scouser in the history of mankind and will forever be known by Liverpool supporters as our own 'Kaiser'. But for me he will always be remembered as the reason why I'm a comedian today.

Funny that.

A LOVE LETTER TO A LIVER BIRD

From the moment I stepped into Liverpool I felt this strange feeling begin to wash over me. I was excited by the sights and the sounds and welcomed by the people. I was part of a very special time in the history of Liverpool Football Club, which is something that will stay with me for the rest of my life. As the years went by, Liverpool became a part of me, and I very much hope that I became a part of Liverpool.

It was, is and I believe always will be a magnificent love affair. A passionate, flaming and enduring love affair with an amazing football club, a unique city and a remarkable people. Somewhere deep in these Bavarian bones there will always be a piece of The Pool.

Scientists reckon that when you fall in love funny things start to happen in your brain. Chemicals go berserk and the way you see the world changes. When you look at the object of your desire blemishes become beauty spots, grating accents sound like poetry and irritating habits become cute idiosyncrasies.

They say that this kind of blind love is a type of madness. The parts of the brain that get excited when you are in love are the same areas that scientists have seen to be affected in patients suffering from mental illness.

Yet when you fall 'madly' in love with someone or something nothing can shake your resolve. These days as I wax lyrical about my incredible Scouse adventure, I'll catch people laughing at the way I see the world. For the love-struck see the world differently. On a fine day I find the drive into Liverpool as scintillating as others might find a drive into Milan. Liverpool: the sights, the sing-song guttural accent, the sense of place, the happy-go-lucky comedic outlook, the shabby-chic of the historic neighbourhoods, the iconic buildings, the cultural inheritance, the Harajuku-style fashion sense and, to borrow a line from The Beatles, there's just 'Something in the way she moves'.

If you are suppressing a snigger at this moment then you won't be the first person to do that. Maybe you haven't come under the spell of the liver bird and all that she stands for in the way that I have.

You can laugh if you want to. I am truly, madly, deeply under her spell and that's how I want it to stay. Always.

This whole book is really my love letter to the liver bird – the mythical symbol that represents the mysterious spirit that has captured my imagination and left an indelible mark on who and what I am. It tells the story of how I came to feel a part of a place that I now regard as my spiritual home, and how it's stayed with me on my travels through Bolton,

Manchester and Stockport. I've also included some stories of the days before I became a Scouser, because I'm also a German you know.

It's a love story really, a heart-on-the-sleeve expression of the feelings I have for Liverpool. That may seem like a funny thing for a footballer to put down in black and white. Especially one who was born into a nation more noted for its cold, calculated efficiency than its romance. You might even say it's a bit mad.

But like I said, blind love is a kind of madness.

Walk on.

CHAPTER ONE

THE GEOGRAPHY TEACHER

'In which calamitous clobber transforms Herr
Didi into Didi-Lar'

It started with a suit. Or rather, a collection of garments that
to the untrained eye of a German exiled in the north-eastern
corner of England seemed to be the essence of style and
sophistication.

I like Newcastle. It was 1999 and I was a Newcastle United
player. Yet you would have to say that in the fashion stakes
it really isn't a Milan or a Paris. In that respect I'd go as far as
to say it is not even a Liverpool. In fact the semi-naked Geordie
in sub-zero temperatures says it all.

Though I can have no complaints with the tailors of
Newcastle. I can't blame them for the way I looked when
I went down to sign for Liverpool. I thought that I was
being bold and cavalier as I picked out the jacket that I
would wear. I wanted to look smart and professional. I
wanted to come over as the essence of German efficiency,
reliability and solidity. But I wanted to do it with style. I

1

imagined myself as a kind of walking-talking-footballing BMW.

A rather sensible brown jacket, the type favoured by solid English gentlemen, caught my eye. 'Yes,' I thought. Distinguished, elegant, professional and not too flash.

Then I noticed a nice pair of brown slacks with a sharp crease down the front. I liked something about that sharp crease. It was definitely the sharpness of the crease that did it for me. It sort of smacked of efficiency. Those slacks looked just the thing to go with the jacket. So I announced that I would take them.

For most men shopping can be hard, and I'm one of those men, but once you have bought one thing, then another, it gradually becomes easier. I found myself warming to the task. I became a little nonchalant as I began to see a theme developing, and the white shirt with the brown check pattern proved irresistible.

The salesman must have thought that this was his lucky day, because just as I was about to pay I saw what I thought would be exactly the right accessory for the checked shirt. It was a violently striped brown tie.

I remember hanging these items in the wardrobe and was proud of my afternoon's work. I surveyed them: the sturdy cut of the jacket; the sharp creases in the trousers, I definitely liked those creases; and the contrasting geometry of the stripes and the checks. Perhaps a little self-congratulatory smile spread across my face as I imagined looking up towards the cameras, pen in hand, head slightly tilted, looking as sharp as I had ever looked. They may not know too much about me in Liverpool, I thought to myself, but I was sure that they would be in no doubt that I looked like a professional.

I closed the wardrobe door and waited.

Even with my agent working on a move away from Newcastle United, all of the hype that often goes on around transfers wasn't there. I'd made it clear in the middle of the season that I wanted to leave Newcastle. I was out with an injury and they seemed pretty calm about the idea of allowing me to leave at the end of the season. However, when I came back into the team after Christmas I got into great form and they became gradually more resistant towards the idea of me leaving.

Gerard Houllier at Liverpool had picked up that I might be available but waited until the season had finished before making enquiries. I began to get updates on how things were progressing as he started negotiations with Newcastle. He would ring every two or three days to reassure me, 'Didi, just be patient, you are going to come to Liverpool.'

I definitely liked the idea, but as far as a move was concerned, the season had come to a close and nothing had happened. The summer came and went and still nothing had been finalised. Some players might have gone and kicked the manager's door down demanding a move. That's not really my style.

I took a more low-key approach. When preseason training started I simply did not turn up. Amazingly, not one of the powers that be at Newcastle said anything. There were no calls asking where I was, no threats of fines, nothing. So I just carried on with my low-key approach. It was a little like the way rabbits are when they get startled. They just sit perfectly still and hope that you just melt away into the background. There was no high drama and no rows. I just sat still and waited to see what would happen.

I said nothing. They said nothing. I thought, 'This nothingness must mean something.' It was then that I thought that I should hit the shops. If I was to sign for Liverpool I wanted to look like a proper Liverpool player.

About two weeks into preseason (I still had not checked in with Newcastle), I got the triumphant call from Houllier. I was to be his seventh close-season signing following on from Titi Camara, Stephane Henchoz, Sami Hyppia, Erik Meijer, Vladimir Smicer and Sander Westerveld.

Although this was an incredibly exciting moment for me, I tried to remain calm. A couple of days after Houllier's call, I walked over to the wardrobe and removed the plastic covers from the new purchases. In my eyes I had done myself proud and I thought that the whole outfit worked well together, with just the right combination of the clothes matching and contrasting. One last check in the mirror and I set off for Liverpool to sign the papers. 'Didi,' I thought, 'if BMW were in the business of making people with brown hessian upholstery, they would surely have made you.'

I laugh now when I look at the photo of me signing the contract. At the time I thought that I looked the dog's bollocks.

The *Liverpool Echo* later described me as 'wearing the kind of brown outfit that parents forced their six-year-olds to wear in the mid 1970s'. My teammates later told me that they had all pissed themselves laughing, believing that Houllier, a former educator himself, had signed a geography teacher.

Yet I think it was the outfit that did it. I think that was what began my love affair with all things Liverpool. Had I turned up full of Pierre Cardin panache, I might have been welcomed into the bonhomie of the French contingent that Houllier was assembling. Had I gone for a style more flamboyant than mud-brown, brown check, brown stripes and materials of a more silky texture than sackcloth, maybe the African lads would have been the people who gravitated towards me.

I think it was something about the oddness of my appearance that caught the comic imaginations of that particular brand of dry humour that is uniquely Scouse. It was the home-grown lads that I bonded with early on and still remain great friends with today. Michael Owen, Steven Gerrard, Robbie Fowler and Jamie Carragher immediately took to me and I found that the Scouse way of looking at the world began to seep deep into my pores as if through some form of osmosis.

Maybe my slightly eccentric look gave them a target for their banter. In among these style-conscious young pros I must have looked like Bavaria's answer to Benny Hill. Even Michael Owen, who is as polite and respectful as you imagine him to be, felt bold enough to join in the fun. He reckoned I looked like John Cleese and nicknamed me 'Basil Fawlty'. I'm tall and wiry and actually I do have the knack of getting myself into slightly bizarre situations all of the time. Having only been in England for a year I didn't really get the joke at the time, but the lads liked it so that was OK. Sammy Lee shortened 'Basil' to 'Baz', so for a while 'Baz' became my name. I thought 'Well, I've been called a lot worse things than Baz', so I was happy with it.

I don't know quite how to describe it, but I immediately felt at home in Liverpool. It was instantaneous. I knew that I was born in Germany, I knew that I was German and I was proud to continue to play for my country. Yet something was seeping through me. It was almost as though there was an element of me that felt English. It began to emerge and grow as it was nourished by the day-to-day banter of the Scouse contingent in the squad, who seemed to regard me as one of their own.

We golfed together a lot. Michael Owen and Robbie Fowler were really keen on horse racing, as I was, and so with our football, golf and racing we were together practically all of the time. It's hardly surprising that for me there was never a language barrier. I was surrounded by the guttural sounds of the Scouse accent constantly and people have said that I sound more Scouse than German.

It started with my calamitous clobber and turned into a glorious love affair – but I still reckon the sharp creases in those slacks were the business.

In a way it's strange that I should feel so positive towards Liverpool as the history of Scouse–German relations is not so great. The city was targeted by the Luftwaffe in the Second World War and Scouse comedian Stan Boardman has made a career out of poking fun at what he calls the 'Geeeeermens'. As a result of this an almost inevitable question for any German on Merseyside is 'Was it you that bombed our chippy?'

So before we start, I didn't bomb your chippy or for that matter anyone else's chippy. I might have eaten my fair share of your kebabs and done my bit to keep Liverpool's independent breweries in business. Come to think of it, I also supported a number of your bookmakers, but chippies and bombs were all way before my time.

Stan's been stereotyping Germans since before even Brad Friedel was born. So much so, you almost feel like asking him, 'Was it you that made a career out of stereotyping other nations?' It's a bit like German tourists turning up on Merseyside and asking random strangers, 'Can vee haf tea in yor yellow zubmarine?'

Yet stereotyping happens. It's just a part of life. If you belong to any nation, tribe or group you are inevitably going to come in for some form of stereotyping, yet surely, none more so than the Germans and the Scousers. We have to be the most stereotyped of all stereotypes. The most generalised of all generalisations. Europe's most famous fall guys. It's something that we have in common. We are misunderstood, made fun of and people resent it when we are successful.

Maybe that was another thing. Maybe that's what bound me together with the Scouse contingent. Despite our relative geographical positions, we have the same burden to bear. People like to poke fun at us and the more successful we are the more irritating it is for them. Germans and Scousers have to grow up with thick skins. Maybe deep inside we share this siege mentality of us against the world. It is nothing to do with the colour of our skin and all to do with the thickness of our skin. Without any effort at all I was being transformed from Herr Didi to Didi-Lar, the Mark I German Scouser.

What is a German Scouser anyway? Someone who always gets the best sunbed but leaves their shell suit on all day? Someone who will beat you on penalties and then steal your football? Someone who . . .? Or maybe I'd better calm down, because that's stereotyping two groups that bear the brunt of more than their fair share of banter. It's worse than stereotyping, because stereotyping two groups is stereotyping in stereo, and I wouldn't want to do that.

As I started to feel more and more at home in Liverpool I began to widen my horizons and take in the whole of the English culture. It's the English way of life that really appeals to me. Things that you may take for granted, are things that I see with an outsider's spectacles on. I'm still a loyal German, make no mistake, but over the years I have become a total Anglophile. I think it is true that I speak with something of a Scouse accent, so maybe you should try reading this as if you are a cross between John Bishop and Boris Becker, and you will be there or thereabouts. These days I even dream in English. Can you imagine that? Seeing myself take the first penalty in the Champions League final wearing plus fours and a deerstalker?

Then there is cricket. Your quaint little English game has become a major passion in my life. I just love the whole thing – the setting, the beer, the eccentric rules, the numbers. I'm a big numbers man, but more about that later. I've even played cricket a few times for the second XI at my local cricket club in Alderley Edge. I'm hoping that now my football-playing days are behind me I'll be hearing the sound of leather on willow more regularly. Perhaps it's better that I don't report my successes on the cricket field to date. My batting performances so far have been hampered with spectators shouting 'duck'. I obligingly bend down and then my innings seems to be over. I'll get the hang of it eventually. I'm told that the club chairman was furious the day I went out for my very first innings. Not because I was dismissed for a duck, but because I had the audacity to enter the crease wearing golf shoes. Apparently this is not the done thing. I guess he was too far away to appreciate the sharp crease in my trousers. To coin an English phrase, 'Things will get worse before they get better'.

My Anglophile tendencies really came to the fore when I was recently given the opportunity to choose from an array of books on all sorts of subjects. I'm a big sports fan of course but tend not to read sports books – though I may read this one. I instantly saw the book that I wanted to read. It was *Churchill Defiant: Fighting On 1945–1955*. A strange choice for a German you might think. A bit like Jamie Carragher having a copy of *Mein Kampf* sticking out of his duffel-coat pocket. Carra's probably checking his pockets right now thinking he's got the remains of a Chinese takeaway in there.

I'm a tremendous admirer of Churchill – that's the statesman and orator who led your lot through the Second World War and won a Nobel Prize for literature, not the nodding dog who is trying to sell you car insurance. Just reading about him fills me with an even deeper sense of connection with England and Englishness.

This idea that a German should fall for the old enemy seems unfeasible. I've been called a paradox. At first I thought it was some kind of detergent, but as a footballer you get called names all the time. At least you can print 'paradox'.

I suppose it's a useful word to sum up my life so far. It's

been full of contradictions. I've always been something of a smoker and a pretty decent drinker yet I've had an amazing career through a time when footballers reached athletic peaks never before seen in the game. I think I'm reasonably intelligent and level-headed when it comes to thinking about the game and how it should be played, yet I came within a millimetre of destroying everything I had ever achieved because I couldn't or wouldn't apply my focus and determination to my off-field behaviour when my life hit a difficult patch. To underscore the topsy-turvy nature of the world according to Didi, you have to say that a cricket-playing German Anglophile is about as likely as Stan Boardman coming up with a new routine.

Can you imagine Stan Boardman not mentioning the 'Geeeermens'? Now that would be a paradox.

So my journey to Englishness all began in Newcastle and even that had a Liverpool connection. King Kenny was getting ready to start his third season with the Geordies. Having got them into the Champions League in 1997 and taken them to the FA Cup final in 1998 it looked like The Toon were going in the right direction.

I'd been at the World Cup in France during the summer of 1998 and by our standards it was not a good one. We crashed out of the quarter-finals, losing 3–0 to Croatia in Lyon.

Earlier that year I'd signed a lucrative five-year deal at Bayern Munich and the smart money would have been on me staying there for the rest of my career. In fact, when I signed the deal I had every intention of seeing it out, yet a few months into it I started to get these feelings of dissatisfaction. They were certainly looking after me well. I had great facilities, I was in a team of internationals and I was well paid.

Yet I didn't feel properly valued. I was an experienced international but I still felt that they saw me as the kid who had come through the ranks. I wanted to be a trusted, responsible and senior member of the squad, but I never felt that I was going to be seen in this light. So, by the time the World Cup came around I was ready to listen to offers from overseas. I fancied either the Premier League or Italy.

Kenny Dalglish came in with a bid of £5.5 million and that was enough for Bayern to agree to let me go. I headed for Newcastle knowing virtually nothing about the place and without even having spoken to Kenny Dalglish. I went with nothing but my schoolboy English, probably not much more than 200 words. It was just enough words to order a pint and engage in some clumsy banter with the barmaid. Today it seems it is sufficient to manage the England football team. That's inflation I suppose . . . or maybe deflation, because that's the feeling we all get every time England tumble out of a tournament.

Newcastle United seem to take a perverse pride in making bizarre decisions and in recent years this has almost become a defining characteristic for the club. The removal of Kenny Dalglish just two games into the new season has to rank as one of their most bizarre. He hadn't even lost a game. Granted we started with two draws, but there was a lot of the season still to go at. There must have been some behind-the-scenes issues going on, but because I hadn't spoken to Kenny before I joined the club I had no idea whether the relationships were stable or otherwise. They turned out to be otherwise.

I never got the chance to see much of Kenny's managerial style at close quarters. He turned out to be the foreplay for the man who coined the phrase 'sexy football'. Before I knew it Kenny was out and Ruud Gullit was in. For me, Gullit's instinct for a soundbite was better than his instincts as a manager. We never clashed, but all that I really remember of him is that he was very quiet. He didn't say very much at all. If this was the way to get sexy football I can only imagine that the bedroom of the Gullit household is a quiet place to be.

I felt that I did all right for Newcastle and even though I got injured very early on in the season I tried to make the best of it. I was helped to settle in by a shell-suited, perm-headed Scouser who would take me out for a pint. Terry McDermott had been a coach under Kenny Dalglish and stayed in the area even after Kenny was sacked. Terry and I were often joined by Alan Shearer at our local pub as I acclimatised to this strange new culture. Those who say that Al is 'Britain's most boring pundit' should go out for a pint with him, or stick a pint in front of him on *Match of the Day*. I always found Al to be a great laugh and very good company.

When I was out for a time with injury I did tell Newcastle United that I would like to move on and they were fine about it. They seemed to have no concerns at all, and the indications were that they would not stand in my way. When I got back into the team I really started to click and we had a great FA Cup run, reaching the final. I played the first half of what turned out to be a very one-sided affair, with Manchester United running out easy 2–0 winners. There was press speculation that I had a falling-out with Gullit at half-time and that he substituted me as a result. There was no truth in that whatsoever. I had really taken a hard knock on my hip bone and was struggling with it so we both knew that it was the right decision for me to come off when I did.

I got a bit of a hard time from the Geordie press and the fans when it became known that I wanted away, especially as I began to hit a level of form that was doing me justice and adding to the overall team performance. There seemed to be a feeling that I was agitating for a move. I wasn't; I had just made it clear that I would like to move on, that's different. I even had my car smashed up by fans who were not very happy with me. But I was quite open with Newcastle. I told them I wanted to go and they seemed fine until I came back from injury and started playing well. This didn't stop the press from claiming that I had threatened to go on strike if I didn't get a move. That was all hype, I was absolutely straight with Newcastle.

I really wanted to be a part of great things again and I couldn't see them happening at St James' Park and I was honest about saying that too. As I was growing up in Germany we didn't get a lot of football on TV and very little of the coverage involved English teams. If there was an English game on television it invariably involved Liverpool. I already had a soft spot for The Reds, so when I heard that Houllier was interested I was delighted. I knew right away that I wanted to go there.

It was a long and protracted wait for the move to

Merseyside, but I had a really special feeling about it as I awaited confirmation that the deal had been done. It was more than the feeling that I had had when I moved from Bayern Munich to Newcastle. It was something quite different. It was something of a higher order of anticipation and excitement. There was a feeling that I was about to make a journey which, though it was less than 200 miles, seemed somehow a journey into another world.

It felt almost as if it was a 'calling'. As if there was something calling me to my spiritual home.

It was the sweet silver song of the lark.

CHAPTER TWO

SPRECHEN SIE SCOUSE?

'Cunning linguist in the dressing room'

To be brutally honest, Liverpool were on their way down. Something had to change, and it had to change fast. Gerard Houllier stopped the slide that would have taken the club not quite into oblivion, but into Premier League mediocrity. For a club with the rich history of Liverpool that's pretty close to oblivion. None of us wanted to go towards mediocrity, and Houllier began to lay down a pattern and an approach that in time was to reverse the decline that Liverpool had found themselves in.

Just as football clubs have defining moments when something tips and its fortunes change, so too do players. There are moments in your life when you stop and look around you. I've been lucky enough to experience some amazing times. I've had laughter, glory and occasionally tears.

Sometimes I stop and ask myself, 'How did that happen? How did I get from there to here?' We all love the idea of instantaneous, overnight success, but in reality that rarely ever happens. Sustained success starts off fairly innocuously. It's barely noticeable, but a set of conditions comes about that creates the possibility of success. Small successes then make other goals more reachable, more attainable and in time an unstoppable momentum gathers pace.

That was Gerard Houllier's contribution to Liverpool. In his unflustered, methodical and determined way, he began to lay down the conditions for the momentum of success to begin. For my money, it was just in the nick of time too. Liverpool had been languishing and another year or two of mediocrity I believe would have seen a steady demise of a great club. They were getting into a downward spiral, which had it been allowed to continue would have seen good players reluctant to come to Anfield, which would have had a corresponding effect on results giving the club even less chance of attracting quality. Who knows how far it could have gone? I wouldn't have been surprised if they had slipped into a comfortable low- to mid-table berth in the Premier League. Big clubs, even Liverpool, are not immune to a collapse in fortunes. Just ask the likes of Leeds United, Manchester City and Southampton, who all sank down the leagues in short order in recent times. Liverpool could easily have met a similar fate, albeit not quite so dramatic.

From that perspective Houllier's influence on the club was seismic. Forget about the way things ended for him at Anfield and remember what he did for the club in its proper context. The *Titanic* was heading for the iceberg and Houllier calmly and carefully took control. There was a lot of raw talent in the squad and Gerard began to meld this with a 'foreign legion' of purchases. Many of them were virtually unknown at the time but were about to become major stars. In the case of Sami Hyppia, who was picked up from little-known Willem II for £2.6 million, an all-time Liverpool great was set to emerge. That has to go down as one of the great bargain buys of the decade.

As well as bringing in and melding together new talent, Houllier began to look inwards too. From the training facilities to the overall ethos and regime, Houllier was leaving no stone unturned in his quest to get Liverpool back on an even keel and going in the right direction.

When I look back now I can see that getting those conditions right and being able to build upon them played a big part in what was possible for the team and for me. I didn't quite realise it at the time, but those were the green shoots of a magnificent adventure.

Houllier had shown his faith in me by bringing me in from Newcastle so I was keen to establish myself in the team. However, because my transfer saga had dragged on I missed that all-important early preseason and I was a little behind when the season started. I'd played for Liverpool for about an hour in a friendly in Belfast against Feyenoord and trained for about ten days before our first league game at Sheffield Wednesday. This wasn't quite enough, but it was all that I could do.

I was delighted to be picked to play in that first game of the season at Hillsborough. I was keen to make my competitive debut for my new team. I clearly wasn't 100 per cent fit, but hey, this was Liverpool and I was in the team. More than that, I wanted to make a good impression in my first game.

It had taken a while for me to establish my worth at Newcastle because of an early-season injury. I didn't want to wait to be accepted in Liverpool. I wanted my teammates and the fans to see me fighting for the cause. I wanted Houllier to feel vindicated that he had worked so hard to get me to Anfield. I was perhaps a bit too hyped up for this game for all of those reasons and in my haste to impress I made a bad decision. I went in for a tackle that if I'd been properly fit I would have probably come out of unscathed. In the event I ruptured my ankle ligaments. Disaster. I was going to be out for about eight weeks. It was almost a repeat of what had happened at Newcastle, only this time it had come in the first game of the season instead of the third.

What a way to start my Liverpool career. It was frustrating, but being able to deal with a situation like this is all part of being a professional footballer. You know that at certain stages in your career you are going to be injured, so you have to develop coping strategies to deal with it. When faced with eight weeks out like I was, some players may go into a depression. Others have been known to eat themselves through the period. I'm lucky, I can eat what I want and never put on weight. Also, an unusual clause in my contract helped me to avoid sitting around moping in Liverpool, which at the time was a foreign place to me.

I don't regard myself as one of those players who was demanding and demonstrative. I didn't have an agent behaving like a Del Boy on speed. I did take the advice of a lawyer though and we had negotiated the right for me to be treated by my own doctor in Germany should I have an injury that required a specialist. This injury definitely did.

I'd come to have great trust in Dr Muller-Wohlfahrt, who had treated me at Bayern Munich and had been the doctor with the German national team. There was a history between us, and of course he knew all about me and my previous injuries. I trusted him and he knew me well, so seeing him was the one thing that I insisted on.

This turned out to be a good move. I stayed in Munich, surrounded by family and friends, until the cast came off. When I went back to Liverpool I was straight into my rehabilitation phase. It meant that I wasn't just hanging around counting the days and when I got into rehab there was a definite goal and an end in sight. I wanted to get back into the team and be part of Liverpool Football Club again.

The recovery was going well, and although I didn't think I was quite ready to play, when you love the game like I do, you want to. I was still eager to show the fans and my team-mates that I was going to be a part of the future. There was a big game coming up, because regardless of relative league positions games against Everton are always big games.

I'd become aware of the legendary derby games between Liverpool and Everton. It's one of the world's great derby rivalries and I really wanted to taste the atmosphere for myself. There were just a couple of hours to go before the game with Everton and I was sitting in my room with my foot in a bucket of ice. There was a knock at the door. I opened it, it was Gerard Houllier. 'Didi, you are playing today, OK?' he said, more as a statement of fact than a question.

I hesitated for a moment and I was about to query the decision when I stopped myself. 'I've come here to play,' I thought, 'and he wants me to play so that's what I'll do.' I looked down at my foot, it was a bluey-white colour like a frozen piece of Stilton; then I looked at Houllier and said, 'Yes. Great. Thanks.' I was delighted and excited, yet in the back of my mind I was a bit anxious about the injury. I placed my foot back into the bucket of ice and began to think about the Everton game.

Partially fit and carrying the remnants of an injury wasn't the best shape in which to take on my first Merseyside derby. Everton came to our place on this occasion, in what turned out to be a disastrous day all round.

After just four minutes Kevin Campbell slipped the ball under Sander Westerveld to put the visitors one up. In that short time I realised that Houllier had made the wrong decision in picking me and I had been wrong not to question him. I now wondered why I had not queried his decision. Yet there I was on the pitch in an intense game that could only become even more intense. 'Oh fuck,' I said to myself. 'How am I going to get through this game on one leg?' We were struggling to reply and as the game went on my ankle injury became progressively worse to the point where I was in absolute agony. I could barely put my foot on the floor and I had to leave the field after sixty-six minutes before what had been a vigorous encounter erupted further. Steven Gerrard came on in place of me, but not for very long. In the seventy-fourth minute our keeper, Sander Westerveld, got into a tussle with Everton's Francis Jeffers. Sander got up and slapped Jeffers, who then slapped him back. They continued trading slaps in this manner as if they were part of some peculiar Merseyside folk dance. The referee had no alternative but to send both of them off. With all of our substitutes used up, Steve Staunton had to go in goal. Things were hotting up and in frustration Steven Gerrard launched a waist-high tackle on the scorer, Campbell, and got his marching orders. We ended up with nine men, an outfield player in goal and me looking at more time in rehabilitation, just sitting on the sidelines. As derby games go, they don't come much worse than that one. The Liverpool fans must have looked at me and thought that Houllier had bought a 'dud'. I was angry with myself more than anything. I realised that there are times to be a hero and times when you just have to say 'I can't help this time.'

From a playing point of view things were not starting well for me at all. Still, I could not have been happier than to be in Liverpool. There was a jaunty feeling about the place wherever you went and everyone seemed to be an apprentice comedian. I liked to go for a pint in the pubs and just watch people and listen to the things they were saying. I suppose it's a bit like being on holiday in another country, where everything and anything seems interesting and novel. Sometimes I'd just stand at the bar and simply listen to the casual conversation. I'd try to pick up on the jokes that flew around and took great delight in listening to the distinctive sounds of the Liverpool accent. I was improving my grasp of the English language and I was seeing ordinary English life, so as well as this being a good way to wind down, it was also research into the culture if you like. My very own self-imposed homework in the pub.

As I became an established player I obviously found that I was recognised more and more wherever I went. I had absolutely no problems with that at all. I will always shake someone's hand, pose for a photo with a fan and have a chat if that's what people want to do. I've always been happy to oblige. Although a lot of the money in football now comes from TV deals, the fans are still paying their hard-earned money every week to come and watch. No matter who the legal owner of a club is, a club belongs to the fans, particularly a club like Liverpool. Owners may come and go, but if you are a Liverpool fan you are a fan for life. The fans bring the passion, and their contribution to our wages is a big deal for them. I've always been conscious of this and appreciative of it, so there has not been one occasion where I have tired of engaging with the fans.

There are times though when you just want to have a quiet pint. That's pretty normal. You need somewhere where you can sit and study the *Racing Post* or watch a televised match in quiet anonymity just like everybody else does. When you are a Liverpool player in a soccer-mad city that's not easy. So I thought to myself, 'Where can I go for a quiet hour or two?' I knew that if I went to a pub favoured by Liverpool fans that I would certainly enjoy it, but I wouldn't be able to settle into a bit of quiet rest and relaxation.

It seemed obvious to me. My theory was that if everyone wanted to talk to me in a 'red pub', then surely nobody would want to talk to me in a 'blue pub'. That's how I became a regular frequenter of Everton-friendly pubs. I would walk in, order my drink and there would be the occasional bit of banter across the bar, but no more than that. If that happened it was all very good-natured. Nobody wanted to shake my hand or talk about last Saturday's game and it would have been sacrilege for any of them to want a photo. There was no abuse either strangely enough. I would be left alone to read my paper, watch a match or just be alone with my thoughts.

That's the funny thing about Liverpool and Everton. Although the rivalry is intense and at times bitter when they are up against each other, there seems to be a quiet respect for each other as well. Some people may think that I was crazy and that I was walking into the lion's den by going into a 'blue pub', but in all the years that I did that I never had a single moment of trouble. Today you hear of foreign players struggling to settle down, even saying they dislike the city in which they are paid unbelievable money to play. I would say that they should take a reality check. Don't live like a prima donna in a gilded cage. Go and do the things that normal people do. Enrich your life and be a part of the culture, not a prisoner of it.

By February 2000 I had begun to establish myself in the team and when we played Leeds United at home I scored my first Liverpool goal after just nineteen minutes. It was a memorable game for me, not least because we won 3–1 and I scored, and it was a memorable game for the referee too. When Patrik Berger scored our second goal, referee Mike Reed was caught on camera pumping his clenched fist in the air and crying out 'Yes'. You would have thought that he had scored the goal rather than Berger.

Was he a closet Liverpool fan unable to contain his delight any longer? According to Reed he was elated because he had played the advantage rule instead of blowing up for a foul on Vladimir Smicer in the build-up to Berger's goal. He reckoned that having made a big call, he felt vindicated by the fact that we had scored and that he was simply pleased with himself.

That win against Leeds United turned out to be an important one in the context of the whole season. As it came to the final run-in it was tight at the top and at that time there were only three Champions League places available to English clubs. Leeds United were in third place in the table, with us chasing them hard in fourth place. We knew exactly what we had to do. If we could win our last game of the season at Bradford City, who were fighting to avoid relegation, and Leeds got a draw or less, we would qualify for the Champions League. That would be a mighty achievement and a sure sign that after years in the doldrums Liverpool were making progress. We had every reason to believe that we could go to the relegation-threatened Bradford City and win.

Bradford City of course were fired up and fighting for their Premier League lives. For some reason we were misfiring on all fronts and seemed strangely impotent. Chances for us were few and far between and I conceded a free kick against Gunnar Halle, which was floated into the box for David Wetherall to score almost unopposed. We lost 1–0.

Leeds United drew, so the Champions League had been within our grasp if only we had been able to do the business at Bradford City. It was a devastating end to a season. We were genuinely heartbroken to be so close and yet so far. But looking beyond the disappointment it meant progress for Liverpool and a place in the UEFA Cup the following season.

Houllier's medicine was working and the patient that was Liverpool Football Club looked to be on the mend. To be fair things probably worked out better for us in a funny sort of way. We were not yet geared up to make a serious assault on the Champions League and the UEFA Cup gave us a chance to win our spurs in Europe as Houllier continued to refine his formula.

During the close season that followed, Houllier continued to bring in more foreign signings and by now a sizeable French contingent was making its presence felt in the changing room in preparation for the 2000/01 season. He obviously had a very good grasp of who was who in the French leagues and he wanted to use this to his advantage by picking up players that may have gone unnoticed by other clubs.

This was definitely not a case of Houllier surrounding himself with his fellow countrymen in order to make himself feel more at home. He wanted to create an integrated team and went to great lengths to ensure that everybody, regardless of nationality, obeyed one of his golden rules. 'The moment that you step into the training ground or the dressing room the official language is English' he frequently had to remind players. I had no difficulty with this even when fellow Germans Markus Babbel and Christian Ziege joined. I was comfortable with English and felt no desire to have conversations in German. The French players would sometimes slip into the habit of speaking among themselves in their native tongue, and Houllier took them on a couple of times during our team meetings. Eventually he tired of having to remind them of the rule and he told them very forcibly in English, 'If I find you speaking in French one more time, you will be out of the door the next day.' It seemed to me that Houllier was much harder on the French players about it than he was with the other nationalities.

The one person you would not expect to break the language rule was Houllier's assistant Phil Thompson. If you have watched him on Sky TV you will know that when Thommo gets excited he even struggles to make his English comprehensible. At times it's like watching an Esperanto speaker with a mild case of rabies as he tries to describe what he is seeing on his monitor.

People have differing views about Thommo. Houllier was definitely the studious, reflective type, while Thommo was the polar opposite. Houllier was the carrot while Thommo I think was brought in to be the stick. I don't know if he had been given that precise brief or whether he even realised that he was doing it, but he was definitely the 'stick', brandishing pain wherever he felt it was deserved. His tirades against players who he thought were underperforming were legendary. His hands would fly all over the place to emphasise the points that he was cursing about. He looked rather like a cage fighter with a bad case of Tourette's.

To understand Thommo and the way he is, you have to realise that first and foremost he is a Liverpool fan. He just happens to have played in some very successful Liverpool teams and been assistant manager and acting manager. But underneath that he is a passionate, dyed-in-the-wool Liverpool-mad fan. He always was and he always will be. He'd had an amazing journey from dreaming of glory while standing on the Kop as a kid, to lifting European Cups.

That's why sometimes his passion got the better of him.

His rants and his raves were often knee-jerk reactions of the sort that a frustrated fan might let out at home or in the pub. Instead of kicking the cat like the average fan might do, Thommo had the opportunity to kick the player who he was most frustrated with. Because of his position as assistant manager, Thommo was a fan who could let out his frustrations there and then in the dressing room and in the face of the person he was most frustrated with.

This was sharply illustrated in my second season at Liverpool. We were away at Southampton's old ground, The Dell, and winning 3–0 with just seventeen minutes of the game remaining. We were coasting towards a win in a game that we had totally dominated. We deserved to be 3–0 up and it seemed that the points were in the bag. Yet inexplicably we conceded three goals in that crazy seventeen-minute period to come away with only a point. That was a calamitous collapse by anyone's standards. It was not something that Thommo was going to allow to pass without comment.

As we trudged back to the dressing room, obviously we were all disappointed, sick even. Walking up the tunnel you could see that Houllier was down and deeply disappointed to say the least. I looked over at Thommo and it was clear that he was more than just disappointed, he was absolutely incandescent with rage. He was fuming as a coach and furious as a fan. As I saw him charging towards the dressing room his nostrils were flaring and I remember thinking that I'd better get out of the way. He had that look about him. He was definitely going to take someone's head off. There was going to be a ding-dong at The Dell.

As Thompson reached the dressing room he pointed at

Markus Babbel and absolutely let rip. He was really screaming. 'You pulled out of a tackle, that's why they scored,' he shouted. Babbel was one of the new signings that summer and his English was still a bit shaky but he had picked up a few swear words.

He turned around and it took him a moment to understand what had been said. He paused, trying to decipher this rabid Scouse–Esperanto rant. When Thommo's accusation registered with Markus he shouted back at Thompson, 'You mean me?'

Thompson's decibel count got even higher as he repeated his allegation. 'You pulled out of a fucking tackle, that's why they scored.'

Babbel, unsure of how to handle the situation and racking his brain for appropriate English words, got even louder. He was shouting, but in the stilted way that you would expect of a robot. It was like Arnold Schwarzenegger speaking through Professor Stephen Hawking's voice synthesiser with the batteries running low. 'Fuck – off – you – are – ze – shit – house,' he shouted over to Thompson. The slow and thick German accent gave it almost a comedy element that would have caused a laugh under any other circumstances.

With Thommo about to burst a blood vessel you had to think that Markus had made an inappropriate choice of words to say the least. At this point Thommo surprised us all. As a former England international he showed that he had done his homework when it came to hurting the opposition. 'You are the schizenhousen,' he screamed. The uncompromising defender showed he was also a cunning linguist. You sense that he had used that particular German word a few times during his international career.

Babbel didn't need to pause to understand this one. Thommo's insult registered immediately and Babbel's boot flew through the air like a howitzer shell in the direction of Thompson. It missed but the thud of the boot against the wall left us in no doubt that it was more serious than a bit of horseplay. Suddenly Thompson and Babbel were head to head and being separated by an unflappable Houllier. Gerard was always very measured and even in this heated atmosphere he straightened his jacket and tie and simply said to Thompson, 'Sit down and be quiet. We will talk about this on Monday morning.' Amazingly Thommo did as he was told. He sat there huffing and puffing. His face had turned the colour of an Englishman on his first foreign holiday and a small vein in his forehead throbbed like a little neon sign outside a Benidorm nightclub.

When it all calmed down, it was difficult to know which was the more surprising – Thommo speaking German or Houllier not picking him up for breaking the English-language-only rule.

Houllier almost always applied his Monday-morning rule. He might be fuming inside, disappointed or elated, but he preferred to wait before delivering his verdict on situations. Even situations involving a temporary breakdown of Anglo–German relations of the kind he had with Thommo and Markus Babbel.

In the midst of chaos reigning, as it did in the dressing room that day, Houllier always seemed able to remain calm. However, even he showed a small glimmer of anger following that dreadful capitulation at Southampton. Steve Staunton had come on as substitute with nine minutes left and we were still 3–2 ahead. Steve must have thought that he had been put on to try to make an impact and with just a couple of minutes left he gathered the ball about forty yards out and lashed it wide. The Dell was an old-fashioned kind of ground with low-level stands and even though Steve's shot was so far off the mark it almost went out of the ground, it hit the top of the stand and bounced back towards the Southampton keeper who quickly restarted the game. Southampton took possession and immediately went upfield to score a last-minute equaliser. All we had to do was run down the clock, go for the corner flag and just hold posses- sion, but Steve went for a killer punch from a most unlikely distance. It was a poor decision compounded by the fact that we were unable to cling on for the win.

Houllier in his own way was livid. He said quite calmly, 'That is the closest I have ever come to hitting a player.' I guess that's the football equivalent of making a saint swear because Gerard always showed great self-control. In later life Gerard unfortun- ately suffered serious heart problems and showed a tremendous strength of spirit, bravery and a commitment to the cause the like of which I have never seen. I have no idea if his health problems are genetic or not, but I'm sure the fact that he held everything in didn't help. Football can be stressful, for managers more than anyone else, and it's probably a healthy thing to let some of it out every so often.

On that basis Thommo should live to be 178.

Naturally, Gerard did not approve of alcohol. What manager would? I continued to take a drink, not because I was a rebel, but because I thought that I knew my body better than anyone else. I'd always have a bottle of wine or two on a Saturday after a game and even during the week. I felt that an important thing for me was being able to feel relaxed. I always had a very good level of fitness and I always knew if I needed to get a bit of a sweat on. So physically, and I know that sports scientists will howl either with laughter or disgust when I say this, I don't think the drinking and smoking had much of an effect on me.

That's not because I'm special or some freak of nature, I just think that it's because my game was more about thinking about what I was doing than running myself into the ground. I had more than a sufficient level of fitness to play at the top level and I proved that over many years. I knew that if I concentrated on my positioning in the way that I had been taught by great managers, most especially Giovanni Trapattoni, I would perform well for the team. It's no secret that I didn't have a great turn of pace. In fact I was the only player I know that could run faster going backwards than I could forwards. I even heard that sections of the Anfield crowd ran a sweepstake on what minute I would break out of the centre circle and when I would break into a full-blown run.

But that was my game and if I was relaxed as well as focused on what I was there to do, I found that I could perform better. And there was nothing more soothing than the occasional bottle of red for helping me to stay in tip-top condition.

Of course Gerard had banned alcohol from the players' lounge. He didn't want players coming straight out of a game and refuelling with alcohol. That didn't stop Robbie Fowler from showing his support to our shirt sponsor Carlsberg.

There was a time when Robbie Fowler was going through a frustrating period with injuries and he wasn't playing as much as he would have liked. He hated that period and on the day he eventually got back into the team he struggled a bit. He just couldn't get into the game and he was pulled off at half-time. Furious with himself and at the substitution, he went straight into the showers and got changed. Obviously he couldn't get a drink in the players' lounge, but this kid was streetwise and knew the nooks and crannies of Anfield as well as anyone. He made his way through to the Carlsberg Lounge, a hospitality area just around the corner from the players' enclave where, since Houllier had arrived, prohibition reigned.

After the match we were getting ready in the dressing room and as we were all chatting I noticed Robbie staggering towards us. I thought, 'He looks a bit the worse for wear.' As he got closer I said to Carra, 'He's absolutely steaming.' Which in truth he was. There was no mistaking the glazed eyes, the slurred speech and the occasional stumble.

Gerard saw this quite clearly too, but he did not say a word. Despite his distaste for alcohol and the banning of it from the players' lounge, he looked at Robbie with what seemed like the glare of a knowing teacher. It was as if he was thinking, 'Mmmm. I'll see you in the headmaster's office on Monday morning.' It was Houllier's Monday-morning rule in operation again. It seemed that there was nothing that couldn't wait until Monday morning. Looking at Robbie and the state he was in it was going to take him until Monday morning to sober up.

Sure enough when Robbie arrived for training on the Monday morning he was pulled straight into the headmaster's office and Robbie received his reprimand. But there was little Gerard could do when we were away from the training ground and I don't think he ever took into account the bonding effects of the lads having a few bevvies together.

For example, we were out one night soon after I first arrived and I think they were expecting a German to be quite sensible. We had all had a few and Carra and co., despite their fame, were having a hard time pulling a taxi home. I was a bit merry by this stage and so I announced that I would organise a lift. They looked at me with a mixture of confusion and horror as I lay down in the middle of the road and closed my eyes. I heard a car coming in my direction, gritted my teeth and hoped for the best. The car screeched and came to a halt in front of me. I got up and went over to the driver.

'I'll give you fifty pounds if you take me home,' I said.

The driver looked at me a bit suspiciously and then said, 'All right pal, where do you live?'

My cockiness turned to embarrassment when I realised that I couldn't remember my new address. For the lads that were with me that night, their perception of Germans had changed for ever. There is no doubt in my mind that these social sessions we had did a lot to bind us together as a group, and there was one memorable moment when I took that feeling of togetherness a little step further.

We were on a preseason tour and Joe Corrigan was our goalkeeping coach. Joe is a big fella and, as Manchester City's goalkeeper, had put his head where it hurts a few times more than was good for him. Consequently he had developed a permanent look of being battered and bruised. With his hair thinning and his body slightly bulking out he wasn't exactly looking his best. We were all having a few drinks and as my eyes glazed a little and my tongue loosened, Joe's face began to look ever-more bizarre with each drink that I put away. I don't know why, but I turned to Joe and said, 'Joe, you are the ugliest man I've ever seen.' Before he could respond I put my arms around him and gave him a big smacker on the lips.

I think that was my survival instinct kicking in. He was a big lad and I quickly needed a way to diffuse the insult that I had just given him. It gave everyone a laugh, including Joe thankfully, and it was just another incident that helped us establish a real team spirit.

Whenever there was laughter and merriment at Liverpool, on the pitch or off it, nine times out of ten there was one person at the centre of it all. He was the one guy that made me laugh more than anyone else, and he still does.

Of all the great comedians that Merseyside has produced over the decades – Ken Dodd, Stan Boardman, Alexei Sayle, John Bishop, Tom O'Connor, Kenny Everett and so the list could go on – there is one unsung hero in the comedy stakes. I'll introduce you in a moment to the funniest Scouser never to perform on stage. He is the Cultural Attaché for Bootle.

CHAPTER THREE

THE CULTURAL ATTACHÉ FOR BOOTLE

'Strange stories of time tunnels, Tokyo police and a Bulgarian piano player'

Jamie Carragher probably won't even remember how he first introduced himself to me. I definitely do. It was at St James' Park on 30 August 1998 and I was a Newcastle United player. After Kenny Dalglish had been sacked as The Magpies manager Ruud Gullit took charge of his first game, promising to bring his brand of 'sexy football' to the north-east. That first game was against, of all teams, Liverpool.

I knew that at the time Liverpool had a lot of good young lads coming through, though to be honest I didn't know very much about them. I didn't have the luxury of observing them for very long either as the game kicked off at a high tempo. There was no room for foreplay in this new sexy football regime. It was a feisty game right from the start and early on Gary Speed clattered Liverpool's hardman Paul Ince to really test out Ince's suspect ankle. That set the tone, and I had my first big call to make as early as the twelfth minute of the game. That's when the young Carra introduced himself to me. The ball sprang loose and there it was, equidistant between me and him. There was precious little time to think. We both went for it hard and at the last moment I pulled back a little. Carra, as is his nature, did no such thing. He went straight in and took the ball cleanly. I, meanwhile, suffered. I could immediately feel that something was wrong. While I hobbled about trying to see if I could shake off the effects of his bone-crunching tackle, Carra carried on unaware that I had damaged my medial ligaments. Soon after I limped off and spent six weeks on the sidelines. In the match the only sexy football seemed to be coming from Liverpool. Michael Owen produced a knee-trembling fifteen-minute first-half hat-trick as we were crushed 4–1. Pleased to meet you Mr Carragher.

By the time we went down to Anfield for the return fixture I had no ill feelings towards the lad, but his name had hit the headlines for all the wrong reasons. Tabloids had been tracking the Liverpool players during their Christmas party and there was some story of off-the-pitch sexy football. Carra had got embroiled in a bit of a scandal that had hit the newspapers the day before the game. What I remember is that as he came on to the pitch he was given a rousing ovation by the Liverpool fans. He was Liverpool through and through and they wanted to let him know that they supported him as a player irrespective of the rights or wrongs of what had happened off the pitch.

It was another Liverpool nightmare for me. We were playing well and leading at Anfield 2–0, which is not a position too many teams get into. But I just couldn't seem to stay on the field against Liverpool for long enough to make an impact. I committed a foul on Steve McManaman. It was bad and I was lucky to get away with just a yellow card. Perhaps Patrik Berger felt a sense of injustice because when I went near him, although I did make contact, he half-dived to ensure that I would play no further part in the game. I was off the pitch again against The Reds.

Liverpool stepped up a gear and incredibly turned a 2–0 deficit into a 4–2 win in the final half an hour. So it is that Carra became associated with two Liverpool encounters that were not the best for me, even though he was totally unaware of it. His name had lodged in my mind.

From the moment I arrived at Anfield I took to him. Few people can really make me laugh, but Carra seemed tuned to my frequency. It was a bit like when you are searching for a radio station that you like. All the other noise in the dressing room seemed like static to me until Carra walked in and suddenly it felt like my favourite radio station was coming through loud and clear. There was something about his attitude, the way he said things and of course the things he came out with.

The thing that you quickly notice about Scousers is how proud they are of everything that is Liverpool. Carra is no exception to this rule and soon after my arrival he took it upon himself to widen my knowledge of the great city of Liverpool. He was like the Cultural Attaché for Bootle.

We were getting dressed in the changing rooms after training one day and Carra caught me as I was coming out of the shower. He did that thing that Scousers often do. They prepare you for a question by making a statement first but making it sound like a question. Then they ask you the question. So Carra looked at me and said the question-like statement, 'Eeaaarrr Didi?' Then the question, 'Fancy coming up my neck of the woods today?' I didn't think twice about it because I do like a good laugh, and here was one of the few people I've ever met that can really make me laugh out loud. I have a certain sense of humour that tends not to be turned on by the obvious. There was something about Jamie Carragher from the outset that just clicked with me. He has a funny way of looking at the world and I always knew that when I was with Carra I would find myself laughing.

'All right,' I said, like the innocent abroad, 'where's your neck of the woods?'

'Bootle,' replied Carra. 'It's sound.'

I'd been around the Scouse contingent long enough to know that 'sound' had nothing to do with the decibel level of the local nightclubs, but could be used to indicate a high degree of approval of anything from soft toilet tissue to a political ideology. From his enthusiasm I felt that we must be heading for Liverpool's equivalent of a Los Angeles hip neighbourhood. That sounded like it might make for a pleasant day out so I followed Carra's lead and we set off for Bootle. You could see as we drove through the streets that the lad hadn't travelled very far in terms of distance from Bootle to Anfield, but the gift of being a great footballer was something that had taken him into another world. I didn't catch the name of the town that Bootle is twinned with as we passed the sign, but had Carra told me it was battle-torn Beirut I would probably have believed him. With the greatest of respect, this was definitely not Liverpool's Santa Monica. It was a tough neighbourhood, you could get a sense of that immediately. Yet I could see the pride in his eyes as he talked and it was clear that he had lost none of his deep affection for his birthplace. This tough, run-down patch of Merseyside was a part of him as much as he was a part of it.

We pulled into a potholed tarmac car park surrounded by concrete and brick constructions. He was excited as he announced, 'Come on, I'll take you into Cornelius's place.' I thought maybe there was some trendy off-piste little bijou lounge that he knew of around there.

He led the way. We went through a little battered door into what can only be described as a small, dark room. That is the only description I can give you. It was simply a small, dark room. There were a couple of tables, a few shabby chairs, a jukebox and a small bar. That was it. It looked like it had seen better days, and it was almost as if we had gone through a secret door and ended up in a cellar pub in the docklands of Odessa or Gdansk sometime around 1972.

Yet for Carra, it was not about the surroundings. As an emerging young professional footballer he was getting used to having the best of everything. He could have gone anywhere and done anything, yet he chose to take me to Cornelius's. For Carra it was about the people, and I have to say they were really lovely people. Bear in mind though that I was with the biggest thing ever to come out of Bootle and I was known as a Liverpool player myself. Had things been different and I had been a stranger in Bootle it would be easy to see that, to an outsider, this could appear to be an intimidating place.

My eyes hurt as we emerged from the darkness of our little time tunnel into the bright light of the day. I already liked this fella. I liked him even more when I saw the grounded, down-to-earth ease with which he fitted back into his home turf. He was very humble and never came over as the big-time Charlie. He was one of the lads from Bootle. He just happened to be the one who was able to do what they all would have loved to do – play for Liverpool. They wouldn't let it go to his head, and neither would he.

Carra was a great guy to go out for a few pints with. If I felt down about something the chances were that he did too and if there was one person that could lift my spirits more than anybody else it was the Cultural Attaché for Bootle. In May 2000, we lost a home game against Leicester. They beat us 2–0, fair and square, but we had had one of those really frustrating days when things just didn't click. Back in the dressing room we were really down. It was one of those times when it's hard to put your finger on why things didn't work out. Carra suggested we have a couple in town. A few beers lifted our spirits and Carra had another one of his ideas. 'Come on Kaiser, we'll go down Flares.' It was another one of those time-tunnel moments as we searched out this nightclub that Carra knew of. He might have known where he was going but I was just mystified. It's amazing that anyone ever found it, and I wouldn't be surprised if some people are still trying to find their way home. We seemed to go into Liverpool's equivalent of a Moroccan medina. We were somehow close to town, yet it felt like a million miles away with alleys, passageways and dark cobbles leading off at every angle.

Flares was another one of those 'hole-in-the-wall' night places. Inside it was a little snapshot of the late seventies. There was a disc jockey high up on a platform. I say 'disc jockey' because he actually had proper discs. He introduced the records with ever-increasingly corny segues as he pulled out a black vinyl forty-five rpm version of Abba's 'Super Trouper' from a gaudy cardboard sleeve. The Eagle's 'Hotel California' and The B52's 'Love Shack' transported us to another place and another time.

Everybody seemed to be dressed the part too, with flares, platforms and perms. If I'd known, I could have worn the brown outfit that I came down from Newcastle in. It was so seventies you almost expected to see Hansen, Thompson and Keegan chatting up a few birds in the corner; practising their patter for some as yet unknown future sitting on a sofa in a television studio talking in clichés. It was a total time warp. We had a great time and shook off the frustration of the Leicester defeat.

I don't know if Gerard Houllier was a closet seventies groover or not, but somehow word got back to him that we had been in Flares after the game. Was he enjoying a prawn cocktail, followed by chicken in a basket in some corner alcove, waiting for them to play 'Ca Plane Pour Moi' by Plastic Bertrand, before hitting the dance floor?

I don't know, but somehow he knew. Both of us were called into Houllier's office a few days later. He had all the information. He knew where we had been and what we had been doing, but the rollicking was primarily aimed at me. Carra was a bit younger than me, but it is not as if he was a kid and I was leading him astray.

I was beginning to realise that Houllier had more than a soft spot for Carra. I would go as far as to say that he loved him as if he were his adopted son. This was a case of 'man love' as they call it, not a sexual thing in any way, just one man wrapped up in total admiration for another. Yes, Gerard was mad at both of us, but he was especially mad at me because he had high hopes for his favourite son. Carra was given a token telling-off and allowed to leave, while I remained for the main event. The essence of it was that nothing must get in the way of this lad's glorious future. Maybe Carra was the kind of player that Gerard may have imagined he would have been if he had ever made it as a top-flight professional. However you wrap it up, there was no doubt that Gerard was more worried about Carra's future than mine.

He needn't have worried too much because Carra would never let anything stand in the way of him fulfilling his potential. He will always be up for a laugh but he is an immense professional. He's like one of those little dolls that keep bouncing back up when you knock them over. He's physically and mentally very strong and he'll get up every time he gets knocked over.

Resilience is something that we have in common, yet we are opposites in one respect – I always had the routine of being very quiet before a game. I'd get changed, read the programme from cover to cover and then I'd sit there for an hour or so, wanting to be alone with my thoughts. I didn't want to talk to people. I used to like to concentrate on the game, to think it through and get myself mentally ready. I suppose I was a footballing Greta Garbo – 'I want to be alone'.

Carra was the total opposite. For him the prematch dressing room was the football equivalent of the Cambridge Footlights. It was an opportunity to perform and he would walk around chatting and think nothing of having the whole dressing room in uproarious laughter just minutes before we were about to walk out on to the pitch. Most times I could tune out, but sometimes his wisecracks even sucked me in. His preparation was to completely lose himself in prematch mirth, and then he would walk on to the pitch and be as full-blooded and committed as anyone. He could switch from clown to clattering tackle in an instant.

Even though Steven Gerrard became the inspirational and highly respected captain, the whole dressing room revolved around Carra. He was the centre of attention and ruled the roost in the comedy stakes. People say that he looks like Scouse comedian John Bishop. It's true, to look at them they could be brothers. They've actually become great mates and to be honest if it came to it I'd be hard pushed to say who is the funniest. Carra, for my money, could certainly consider having a second career in the comedy business. Maybe when he retires he can ask Cornelius if he can find room for a small stage.

Carra had a lot in his comedy locker. He could do the verbal banter, which of course the English lads loved. As the foreign contingent grew he had a new audience to cater for and the practical joke was a useful way of overcoming the language barrier and there seemed to be no limits to how far he would go.

We had a very experienced physiotherapist called Stewart Welsh, who quite rightly was ambitious and wanted to progress in his chosen field. He was with a top Premier League club and so the next step on the ladder for him was to be one of the England team's physios. He made no secret of his ambition, particularly among the lads who were in the England squad. They were in a good position to drop in a word of recommendation on Stewart's behalf, so why not? Carra had clocked this and with his England career blossoming he took every opportunity to listen carefully to the England physio, Gary Lewin, who at the time was also the head physio at Arsenal. He was listening not for the purposes of giving tips to our own guy, he was slowly but surely perfecting the London accent of the Arsenal man.

When he was ready Carra rang up Stewart Welsh, imitating the accent of the Arsenal physio. 'Alwight Stew? Listen, I've been hearing a lot of good fings abart you from the Liverpool lads in the England team. We got this away fixture wiv England. We'd like you to come and join us as part of the physio set-up. Interested?'

Stewart was well interested. It was like he was living the dream. All of his hopes and ambitions were coming true. He was ecstatic and began telling everyone who would listen that he had been chosen for England duty. This was the day of all days for Stewart.

By the time Carra told me about his little scam, Stewart had been home and told his wife and family. I thought this was a joke that had gone too far and I didn't mince my words. 'You bastard, Carra. This is definitely borderline.' I could see the funny side of it of course, but with Stewart having told his family there was a degree of humiliation involved too. Carra flushed a little and gave a sheepish smile. It was the only time I actually saw him slightly embarrassed by one of his pranks. If I'd known he was going to do it I would have tried to talk him down. When he was on a roll with one of his comedy routines he tended not to listen to anybody, but if anybody could have had a chance of stopping him I think it would have been me.

Carra had no choice but to go to Stewart and tell him it was a wind-up. Stewart's reaction is not reported.

Carra is a law unto himself in the comedy department. I can only imagine that it is something in the genes. His dad, Philly, is a well-known character and a twenty-two-carat Scouser. When he played a part in the film *Fifteen Minutes That Shook the World*, his Scouse accent was so thick and incomprehensible that they had to provide subtitles, even though the audience it was made for was primarily Scouse.

I remember when I first encountered Philly. We had gone out to Spain to play against Valencia in the Champions League and I was sitting next to Michael Owen on the team coach. As we approached the ground, the coach eased its way through a sea of red as some 5,000 Liverpool fans had turned out in great spirits. Michael Owen, who was a pretty calm lad most of the time, suddenly became excited and leaned across me. He was banging his fist on the window. 'Yeeeeeeer. Hey look,' he shouted. 'There's Carra's ol' fella.' I couldn't believe it. Maybe I expected to see a suited gentleman quietly making his way to the ground. In among the thousands of cheering fans there was one man who had been hoisted on to someone's shoulders. He had ripped off his shirt and was leading the chanting, waving his arms in the air and conducting the massed throng as if it were the Last Night of the Proms. This, it appeared, was the larger than life Philly Carragher.

Philly it seemed was well known to the rest of the squad. As soon as Michael shouted out and banged the window, the whole of the right-hand side of the coach stood up and leaned over to the left-hand side to try to catch a glimpse of Philly. It was a good thing we weren't on a boat.

I looked over at Carra thinking that he would be cringing, doubled up with embarrassment at the sight of his dad behaving like a seventeen-year-old. No such thing. Carra was up on his feet banging on the window, making caveman-like sounds and beaming. He was absolutely made up, as everyone else was, to see Philly.

Philly's a ducking and diving type. He goes to every match and even when he hasn't got a ticket somehow he manages to get in. Of course he's followed Jamie's career for England too. For the World Cup campaign of 2006 in Germany, the England team stayed in Baden-Baden and Philly did too. It was another tournament in which England failed to meet expectations and they went out in the quarter-finals on penalties to Portugal. The England party were disappointed but Philly consoled himself with a little souvenir that he brought home with him. Most people would have brought home a German beer stein; an 'I went to Baden-Baden with England and all I got was this lousy T-shirt' T-shirt; or if they were feeling particularly outlandish, a pair of lederhosen. But not Philly. He brought home the Bulgarian piano player from the hotel he was staying in. She came over to live with him in Liverpool. Clearly, with Philly's thick Scouse accent and her speaking a brand of Bulgarian English, there is a bit of a language barrier. I've no idea how they communicate. Subtitles I guess.

Even though Carra has become a massive success and a house-hold name he is still very much one of the lads from Bootle. It was not uncommon when we were travelling far afield to be joined after the match for a few bevvies by some of Carra's old mates. They just seemed to materialise out of thin air as if by magic.

Just as they did the night we had played against the Brazilian team Sao Paulo in the Club World Championship 2005 in Yokohama. We were staying in a hotel in Tokyo, which is a massive city. With a population of 12.5 million people, it's getting on for being twice as big as London. Yet it still has the most efficient transportation system in the world. The subway carries more than seven million people a day and the bullet train is famous for its reliability, so much so that you can quite literally set your watch to the second by it.

But there must be some law of the universe that dictates that whenever a group of Scouse men have had a few bevvies, no matter where you are in the world, no matter how efficient the transportation system, it seems almost impossible to get a taxi. This was the case for us. We had all had a few beers and time was running out. The players had to get back to the hotel in good time to be on the coach for the airport. We would be flying out in just a few hours. A few of Carra's mates tried to sort the situation and after a long time without success finally managed to flag down a taxi. There was a discussion going on and much hand-waving and gesticulation from both sides. Something must have got lost in translation because before I knew it one of the lads had mounted the vehicle and was running across it from the boot, over the roof and on to the bonnet, denting the panels of the car in the process.

Then the efficiency of the Japanese kicked in. I don't know if the driver had a panic button or not, but even in such a massive metropolis it probably took less than two minutes for the police cars to show up, all sirens and flashing lights.

Don't forget, these lads hadn't grown up in a hipster district of Los Angeles, they had grown up in Bootle and they instinctively knew what to do in this situation – run like hell. Which is exactly what they did. They were already out of the traps before someone shouted 'Leg it, it's the bizzies', leaving me standing there with a choice to make.

Even fully fit, I was probably not as quick over a hundred yards as some of Carra's beer-swilling buddies, but I was carrying a knock. Michael Essien had caught me three weeks earlier in a game against Chelsea and I'd only managed ten minutes in the Club World Championship game. Still, when everybody else runs in a situation like that something inside your brain says 'run'. So I ran. But a lot slower than everybody else, and the little legs of the Tokyo police force caught me while everybody else disappeared into the neon Tokyo night.

Down at the police station this was getting serious. Nobody spoke English and I was running out of time. If I didn't get back to the hotel soon I was going to miss the flight. That was going to take some explaining and I'd most probably be docked two weeks wages. That was going to be an expensive fare for a taxi I'd not even taken.

It was a relief to me when the big boss of the police station turned up and spoke beautiful English. I was still wearing my club tracksuit so perhaps he was more lenient than he would have been under normal circumstances. We agreed to a deal. Because there were trainer prints, rather than fingerprints on the taxi, I was to leave an imprint of my trainer and they would release me without charge so that I could get back to the hotel in time.

Meanwhile Carra had made it back to the hotel. By this time he was getting concerned that I wouldn't make it back in time for the airport coach and probably worrying more about how he was going to explain it to the gaffer. Every five or ten minutes he rang my room, only for the phone to be answered by an increasingly grumpy Sami Hyppia, who was my room-mate. Finally, Sami told Carra in no uncertain terms to stop calling. 'No, no, you stop. I sleep now. You know Kaiser he always get back . . . somehow.'

Back at the police station I duly placed my foot where the police sergeant told me to. A quick squelch and I was a free man. I made it back to the hotel with minutes to spare.

As yet, I still haven't heard from the Tokyo police, though I know that as soon as Carra reads this he will be rehearsing his Japanese accent and I should expect a call sometime soon.

DIETMAR HAMANN

That time when we were on the coach going to the Valencia game got me thinking – the moment when Michael Owen spotted Carra's dad in the crowd and all the lads leaned over to one side of the coach shrieking and grunting encouragement while Carra thumped the window and signalled his approval with caveman-like sounds. It was almost primeval. It was as if we the warriors were heading off to hunt bears, backed up by our tribe and suddenly the ancient clan chieftain appeared and the warriors wanted to display their approval.

Perhaps it was some hunter-gatherer gene in Carra's make-up that made him the 'baron of the banter' and the 'prince of the put-down'. When you think about how banter works and why it exists, it probably goes back to Neolithic times when men had to go out and hunt a bear with axes hewn from flint. You couldn't catch a bear and kill it on your own. It required precise teamwork, and the price of getting it wrong or somebody mucking up their part in the hunt was pretty serious – instant death.

Banter, which is predominantly a male thing, probably evolved to bind the group together through humour, but more importantly it is used to prevent any one person from getting above himself. To have one person who feels he is more important than the group can put the whole group in danger. Just as it was with groups of cave dwellers, so it is with football teams. Banter is the lingua franca of dressing rooms throughout the world. There is affectionate, gentle banter that binds the group together, and then there is the subtle and sometimes not-so-subtle art of bringing someone crashing back down to earth with a well-placed put-down. It's all about preserving the cohesiveness of the group.

Carra was brilliant at both types of banter, but he excelled at bringing people back down to earth who he felt were getting 'too big for their boots'. The Cultural Attaché for Bootle went about this as if it was an ancient and prized duty handed down to him through the generations from the hunter-gatherers who grazed their knuckles across the Bootle soil thousands of years ago.

He usually brought people down to earth and back into the group very quickly with one of his cleverly observed put-downs or a carefully timed aside. It was like watching an artist at work. It meant that there was nobody within the squad that put our success at risk by thinking that they were somehow special.

Yet the thing I noticed about Carra is that his desire to humiliate people who went around as if they were big-time Charlies extended beyond the dressing room. He just did not like any form of flashiness.

When a journalist from a national newspaper once asked him how his mates from Bootle reacted to his success he said, 'They took the piss out of me when I pulled my wallet out to pay for the drinks.'

The journalist was puzzled, 'Why's that? Because now you can afford to buy the drinks?'

Carra was deadpan in his response. 'No. It was because I had a wallet.'

He had grown up in a culture where even the possession of a wallet was seen as a symbol of stepping outside the norms of the group, and he received relentless banter the moment he pulled it out. He had been conditioned from an early age not to be flash and flash people could really get

51

under his skin. In the dressing room if someone raised their head above the parapet he would immediately swing into action with an acidic sideswipe or a crashing comment.

Beyond the dressing room there wasn't always the opportunity to rectify the behaviour of flash Harrys who came his way. Sometimes that would get to him a little and he would be frustrated until he could find a way to get it out of his system. Obviously Carra and I were great mates. I was also mates at the time with a guy called Kev Seed, who was a bit of a celebrity in Liverpool. He had the top radio show a few years back, *The Kev Seed Breakfast Show* on Radio City, which had a huge following. Even if you didn't listen to Kev Seed in the morning, if you lived in Liverpool you certainly knew who he was.

I could sense early on that Carra was not that keen on Kev, even though he was a mate of mine. The clues for Carra's coolness towards Kev were all there really. Neither Carra nor I were ostentatious or showy, we just weren't that interested in that sort of thing. Kev though was quite different. He was loud and brash and he liked to be seen and photographed with all the right people. He was a walking self-publicity machine. On top of this he drove a purple BMW convertible with his own personal registration 'K 5EED', and later put it on a Bentley. He would park his car in front of nightclubs so that he could make sure he was noticed.

Kev being an Everton fan didn't bother me either, but I don't think it helped Carra to warm to him. Despite Carra's distaste for Kev I know for a fact that he listened to him on the radio on the way to training every day. That must have wound Carra up even more because Kev's patter usually consisted of 'Heeeey. Guess who I was partying with last night?' He nurtured this 'I'm a celebrity' attitude and his name-dropping became legendary to the point that he was either admired or ridiculed. People had very definite views on how they felt about Seedy.

He'd do things like making sure the press knew he was going to get engaged to his girlfriend, a former Miss UK. He took her to a hotel room and set off an eighteen-foot firework display and had the words 'Will you marry me?' emblazoned in the night sky. He got himself parts in Christmas pantos and loved to see his face splashed across posters in a Prince Charming outfit.

One year we went to his house for a Christmas party and as you went into the house there was a giant blow-up Father Christmas. Every time someone went near it a sensor would kick in, music would start playing and the Father Christmas began doing some kind of break-dance. This was funny for the first twenty minutes. As the party wore on, this thing was going off every two minutes as people walked past and set off the sensor. Eventually I got fed up with it. I looked at Seedy and said, 'That Father Christmas has got to go.' He was unperturbed and it seemed like this stunt tickled his extrovert nature, whereas for the rest of us it had become grating. I picked up the giant blow-up Father Christmas, carried it through the kitchen and out through a door to Seedy's swimming pool, where I launched it into the water hoping it would sink. We got on with the party and forgot all about it.

Next time I saw Seedy it was Easter. 'Hey Didi,' he said, 'I'm stuck with a Father Christmas in my pool thanks to you.'

I said, 'What do you mean? Just pull it out.'

Seedy for once was downbeat 'I can't. Somehow it deflated and then filled with water. It's now anchored in the bottom of the pool and nobody can move it.'

I could laugh at all of this, it really didn't bother me. I just felt that Seedy was in the entertainment business and it was about building his own personal brand, whatever that may be. Being seen and being larger than life was all part of his job. I didn't subscribe to it myself but I found that I could get along with it.

Carra tried his best to get along with it too, but try as he might he just couldn't quite feel comfortable about it. Kev was operating in big-time Charlie territory and Carra's Neolithic instincts were making him twitch.

'I don't like all this flash crap – number plates, swanky cars, dancing Father Christmases . . . wallets,' he'd say.

We'd never fall out about it and I'd just say, 'Ah, Kev's OK in his own way, you just have to understand his business.'

This was usually met by a grunt from Carra. It bothered him and I could see that, but he had no opportunity to put Kev in his place.

Every morning on his show, Kev would do his Workplace Challenge competition. This was a phone-in part of the show, where two businesses would compete against each other in a quiz every day. One person from the business was on the phone but you were allowed to have a bunch of other workers who could shout out the answers to the captain. There were no prizes and the idea was that whichever business won the competition that day would come on the show the next day and so on until they were defeated. Obviously, being on the show was like free advertising. The longer a business stayed in the competition the greater the value of the advertising, as people all over Liverpool were hearing the name of your company every day.

A lot of us listened to the show as we drove to the training ground, and it wasn't unusual for the Workplace Challenge to be a talking point in the dressing room.

Sometimes a business would stay in the competition for three days and very occasionally one would make it through five days undefeated. I think it was Cleveland Kitchens that held the record at the time. When Panorama Kitchens went on and made it through a week, we all remarked on it and said that maybe this lot could beat the record. After two weeks they were still there and Carra commented on the fact that the record had been smashed. After three weeks of success for Panorama Kitchens something began eating away at Carra. He was sensing that something was not right here and his finger of suspicion was pointing towards Kev Seed.

When Seedy announced over the airwaves that Panorama Kitchens had completed their fourth week undefeated, Carra came in, fuming. 'Hey Kaiser. The word on the streets is that your mate Seedy has been fitted up with a kitchen by Panorama, that's why he's keeping them on. He's feeding them the answers. The sneaky little . . .' You would have thought that a professional footballer at the top of his game would have other things to worry about, but this gossip that he had picked up in the backstreets of Bootle was adding insult to injury.

Carra's mind was turning. Somehow he seemed to feel that the onus was on him to put Seedy in his place and that the future of the whole human race depended upon it.

Panorama Kitchens remained undefeated for something like forty-two consecutive days, beating the previous record by a country mile. It was an extraordinary performance from a group of kitchen fitters and office staff, surpassing even Liverpool University's efforts by forty days. Seedy fawned all over the new record holders, congratulating them on an incredible feat and mentioning Panorama Kitchens as often as he could. Carra quietly fumed, then let out a barrage of expletives and then you could almost hear his brain turning over. I was caught a little bit in the middle here. I knew that if I was out with Carra and we saw Seedy that he would come over and join us, but I knew that Carra would feel obliged to rectify what he had convinced himself was a wrong. How he would do that I had no idea, but I knew Carra wouldn't rest until he got this off his chest.

By now there was speculation all over town that something about the runaway success of the Panorama Kitchens team seemed a bit dodgy. Forty-two days undefeated just seemed unfeasible and the rumour about Seedy getting a new kitchen had become common currency right across Liverpool. Although no one knew for sure, many people suspected a fix I think.

A week or so after the record-breaking streak, we came out of a nightclub quite early and jumped into a waiting taxi outside the club door. Alongside us was a massive queue of around a hundred people waiting in line to get in. Just as we were about to pull off, Carra put his hand on the driver's shoulder. 'Hold on a minute mate. Who's this walking up to the club?' In truth it was someone swaggering the unmistakable swagger of self-importance, slowing slightly to allow the waiting crowd to notice his presence. It was the larger than life cocksure Seedy. He paused as someone recognised him, and all the waiting people turned their gaze away from our taxi towards DJ Seed.

Carra's timing, always one of his great qualities on and off the field, was impeccable. With Seedy basking in his moment of glory, Carra pressed the button that let the electric window glide down. Then, with the ferociousness of one of his tackles, he thrust his head out of the window and screamed at Seedy, 'How's yer kitchen Kev Seed? You fuckin' snake.' With that the whole crowd erupted with laughter and began cheering Carra's exposé. Everyone knew what Carra was on about. Seedy stood there looking as deflated as his dancing Father Christmas and went from triumphant hero to pantomime villain in the space of a second. I think he got a bigger laugh that night than he had ever had in panto.

For Carra it was an outpouring of frustration built up over the forty-two-day winning streak enjoyed by Panorama Kitchens and a way of bringing someone who he thought was up his own arse crashing down to earth.

In his mind, he had righted a wrong. The self-appointed protector of the humble man had won yet another battle for the latter-day hunter-gatherer tribal people of Bootle against head-up-their-arse individuals like Kev Seed.

Having said that, I still get on with Kev and when we speak to each other from time to time it seems like it was all only yesterday that our lives were punctuated with dancing Father Christmases and the frisson of tension whenever Kev did something that made Carra cringe. I think Kev and Carra were polar opposites. They are both great guys but see things from different perspectives, and that is just the way it is sometimes.

Whether it's Kev Seed or a new guy from Real Madrid, Carra will use the cutting edge of his wit or a razor-like put-down to make sure that they don't threaten the group. It's great to have someone who can do that. While I think on, I've realised that I've mentioned Panorama Kitchens eight, well nine, times now. For Carra's benefit, I'd better point out that it was for the purposes of telling the story and not in any way an inducement or any suggestion that I should get fitted out with a new kitchen. Though I have just moved house and come to think of it . . .

My great love for all things Liverpool was nurtured by the lad from Bootle more than anyone. We enjoyed thrills and spills. He took me to places where tourists never go and showed me the real Liverpool, warts and all. More than anything he made me laugh out loud day after day. All in all, we had an amazing team spirit at Liverpool that contributed in a big way to our success on the pitch. It may have just given us that extra one per cent that can make a big difference at the top level. There's no doubt that a massive part of that team spirit and team ethic was orchestrated by one man – Jamie Carragher. My mate, the Cultural Attaché for Bootle.

CHAPTER FOUR

THE CRASH OF 2002

'In which Houllier goes against his own analysis and dreams come crashing down'

Sometimes if I wake in the night, I often find myself thinking about one particular incident, one particular decision. We should have won the Champions League in 2002. If ever there was a chance to win it, it was then. No matter how many times I go over it, I still come to the same conclusion. The Champions League was within our grasp. We should have won it and it would have been a fitting tribute to the progress Gerard Houllier had made if we had.

I don't want to come across like one of those old pros that are always saying 'We shoulda done this, we shoulda done that.' But there is one incident that I think about that gives me reason to believe it's true. The more I think about it the more I strengthen my belief that we certainly could have and should have won the Champions League that year.

Gerard was never prone to moments of madness, but in his terms I think he had one in 2002. He made an error of judgement that cost us the opportunity of being the European champions.

Gerard and I had a few 'coming togethers' over the years. That's pretty normal and you just get on with it. Our 2002 coming together still rankles me a little.

That year we had done it the hard way. To get to the group stage of the Champions League we had to go through a qualifying round, playing against the Finnish team Haka. It was a 9–1 aggregate win and we went through easily, but you still have to get through and we did.

The group stage was tricky too. We had Boavista, Borussia Dortmund and Dynamo Kiev, all of which were potential banana skins. But we came through unbeaten and topped the group, so we were really beginning to feel positive about our progress. That year the group stage was doubly tricky because there was a second group stage to decide the quarter-finalists. We came through along with Barcelona, by nudging out Roma and Galatasaray.

The Champions League quarter-final put us up against Bayer Leverkusen. No quarter-final tie is easy but as a result of the way we were playing and the way we had come through the group stages we felt that we had as good a chance as any of going through to the semi-finals.

Leverkusen came to Anfield and lined up with five players in midfield, with Michael Ballack orchestrating things. They surprised us and they were playing as if they were the home team. They were brilliant at maintaining possession and it was like being hit by a series of waves as they came at us time and time again.

I felt that we were going to get absolutely battered and

then just a minute before half-time our captain intervened. Michael Owen received John Arne Riise's corner, swivelled and knocked it across the box for Sami Hyppia to prod it home. It was totally against the run of play, but it was a goal and that's what mattered. In the second half they came at us in waves once again and it was all that we could do to hang on. We were defending deeper and deeper into our own half, but somehow we managed to weather the onslaught. After ninety minutes of unbelievably hard graft we were 1–0 winners and still had the meanest defence in the Champions League.

Going into the second leg with such a slender lead we were prepared for yet another onslaught. They came at us with fast, pacy, passing football and after just sixteen minutes I found myself pulled over to the wing, leaving Steven Gerard to pick up the dangerous Michael Ballack. Ballack sold Stevie a great dummy and lashed it past Dudek to make it 1–0 on the night and 1–1 on aggregate. The tie was now balanced and we had work to do.

We were trying to absorb Leverkusen and play counter-attacking football. Heskey had a good chance and Owen found himself in a one-on-one with the keeper but both failed to score. When Danny Murphy found Abel Xavier from a corner we equalised on the night, putting us back in front by half-time.

They made two substitutions at half-time, bringing on Berbatov and Neuville, which signalled their intent to go all out for victory. Michael Owen got into a second one-on-one with Butt, their keeper, and pushed it past him only to see it rebound off a post.

With around thirty minutes to go, as they came at us we were beginning to find ways through to create serious chances of scoring. At 2–1 up on aggregate and with an away goal, I felt that we had every chance of going through. Then I saw the number sixteen being held up on the touchline. I was number sixteen. When I realised I was being substituted I just couldn't believe it. Not that I am immune to substitution, but with the away goal in our favour they had to score another two goals to go through – three in total.

A few weeks before the game Houllier had talked to us. He said, 'I've been looking at the statistics. When Didi is on the pitch we have never conceded more than three goals.' That's not me blowing my own trumpet, those were the facts as analysed by Houllier himself. I was a defensive midfielder so for me it meant that I was doing my job.

As I came over and sat on the bench I began to think about what Houllier had said. 'Surely then,' I thought, 'I should still be out there.' This was a quarter-final of the Champions League after all, and we had an amazing chance to go through.

From that moment Leverkusen just went for it and began to run riot. Three minutes later they were 2–1 up on the night when Ballack charged through to nod home. On sixty-eight minutes Berbatov got the last touch after a goalmouth scramble and scored a third, putting them 3–2 ahead on aggregate.

When Jari Litmanen scored for us in the seventy-eighth minute, pulling it back to 3–3 on aggregate, it looked like we would go through on away goals. We simply had to hang on for twelve minutes.

But this had already been a roller coaster of a game and there was one more twist to come. They threw everyone forward. I sat on the bench feeling impotent. I should have been out there helping and there was nothing I could do.

Six minutes. Just six minutes left, then the Brazilian Lucio sprang the offside trap and put a left-footed drive past Jerzy Dudek.

We were all, to use a cliché, totally gutted. You can imagine. We were in command before my substitution, and Houllier himself had said that we didn't concede more than three when I was in the team. We would have had a semi-final with Manchester United, which we would have felt good about because at the time we had a superior record against them and felt that over two legs we could have made it to the Champions League final. In 2002, that would have been against a Real Madrid team that were beatable and in the final Leverkusen were almost but not quite capable of conquering them. I think that we could have. This could have and should have been our year.

I got a lot of questions from the fans as we left the stadium. People seemed to assume that I was taken off because I was injured. Clearly they felt that the only reason to take me off in those circumstances was because I had to come off. I just told them that I wasn't injured, I didn't know why I had been pulled off and that I didn't feel that I should have been pulled. I was fuming at the time but I'm pretty sure that my comments were measured and were in no way a rant.

Back at the hotel I was in no mood even to eat and went straight to my room. I was still hurting about the substitution and the defeat and as I lay on my bed, the phone rang. 'Didi,' it was the unmistakable accent of Houllier, 'come downstairs. I want to speak with all of you.'

This was strange. It was Houllier's practice to reflect on things and he wanted me downstairs for a chat? This never happened. This was not like Houllier at all. I went down and sat in the hotel lounge on a sofa opposite the boss. All of the players had been assembled and he was straight into us. 'No one speaks about substitutions to the media.' I agreed. Maybe he had picked up that some of the fans had been questioning me about my substitution and thought I was aiming my response towards the press. Though he was speaking to all of us, I couldn't help but think that he was aiming his comments at me in particular.

He continued, 'I will answer all of the questions. You leave that to me. I would do exactly the same as I did tonight if I was in the same position again, so don't you go thinking that I have done something that I regret.'

That just did not ring true with me. Gerard was highly intelligent and he always liked to look back on situations before he would apply the Monday-morning rule and deliver his analysis. Surely in his reflections he would have seen that we had every chance to win and that given an opportunity to change things, he would have left me on.

But I didn't argue the toss at the time. He was stern in the way he put this over and I went along with it. I reassured him that I was not going to whip up a media storm. Yet in the back of my mind I was thinking that this was unusual. Gerard always reflected before speaking about a game, and here he was talking about a detail as soon as we got back to the hotel. Also, he never tried to justify his substitutions to anyone. That made me believe that despite what he had said, he must have felt that he had got it wrong.

I let it pass. Then back at the training ground a few days later I was told that Houllier wanted to see me in his office.

I figured that he was going to pick up where he left off, so I began to get my arguments together.

I was rehearsing it all in my mind. 'Four weeks ago you said that we never concede more than three goals when I play. When we need to avoid conceding you take me off and we ship four goals on the night.' I thought that was a good argument, sound and based on his own logic. Then, for effect I thought that I could add, 'It's not rocket science.' Also, he replaced me with Vladimir Smicer, who was a great guy and a very good player, but he was always more attacking minded. This again seemed like an odd thing to do, so I thought that I would hit Houllier with that too.

I was ready to put him right as I walked into his office and sat down because this was not something that I could forget about. He looked up in his calm headmasterish way and simply said, 'Why did you underperform in Leverkusen?'

'What? Underperform? What do you mean?'

'You were at fault for the first goal,' replied Houllier. 'You were out on the wing when Ballack came inside to score.'

This threw me a bit. I told him that when Michael Ballack pulled inside, Steven Gerrard lunged in and I was out on the wing because I can't be everywhere. That's why we had two central midfielders. Houllier had Phil Thompson sitting beside him and uncharacteristically Thommo remained silent.

Then I remembered that I had rehearsed my arguments, but as I tried to speak I felt my tongue go limp as if it was about to tie itself into a knot. His comment about underperforming had thrown me and really taken the wind out of my sails. I recovered my composure and reminded him of his own analysis. He was having none of it, I could see that, so we concluded the meeting and I left it there. To this day though, I still think that I was in the right.

On reflection I think my first instinct was correct. We all make mistakes, even Gerard Houllier, and this was one almighty mistake. The other thing is that there was something odd about Thommo sitting there not saying a word. That was odd. Had I truly been responsible Thommo's natural instinct would have been to flip me on to my stomach and use me to polish the dressing-room floor while shouting expletives. Thommo must have been briefed to remain silent and support Houllier's thesis. That must have been agony for him.

The bottom line was we had crashed out of the Champions League when we had a golden opportunity to go all the way. I was angry, upset and now chastised like a schoolboy. I sat there and wondered if I would ever again get the chance to taste Champions League glory.

Overall though, Houllier was a very good manager, and I've always felt that quite small things can tip situations one way or the other. It works both ways and Houllier did lay down the foundations for a very successful period in Liverpool's history.

I think one of those small defining moments came in November 2000 in the League Cup at Stoke City's Britannia Stadium. I was actually on the bench to start with, watching the action. We fully expected an uncompromising, physical battle against a Stoke City side that were going strong in the old Division Two, which was the third tier of English football at the time.

One thing that stood out was that Guadalupe goalkeeper Pegguy Arphexad got one of his few games for the first team. He was at Liverpool for nearly two years and only made six starts. He may have been a little rusty or nervous or both, as after only about five minutes Pegguy got into trouble on a back pass. His touch was very heavy and he pushed the ball into the path of an onrushing Stoke City forward.

He had to charge into a fifty-fifty tackle with the Stoke player, which made us cringe on the bench as he crunched in and came off second best. With Pegguy prostrate, the Stoke City player got up and hit the ball against the post. Had that gone in it would have been a different game. Stoke were no easy touch and an early goal would have seen them applying physical pressure.

Apart from Pegguy getting a game though, it was memorable also for the scoreline. We ended up very comfortable winners 8–0 away from home. This just goes to show how small incidents can have a big effect. We came through that game as victors and it set us on a path towards overcoming a psychological barrier and winning a first trophy under Houllier, which in turn set us up for even greater things to come.

We progressed through the rounds and went on to beat Crystal Palace in a two-legged semi-final. The critics said that we had an easy draw, but you can only beat what is in front of you. After losing the first leg at Selhurst Park we went for them good and proper at Anfield and won 5–0.

Unlike some managers Houllier, this particular year anyway,

took the League Cup seriously. I think he thought that he had to get the monkey off his own back and off the back of the club by winning something and this was a real chance to do that.

All that stood in our way was Birmingham City in the final at the Millennium Stadium. You only have to say the words 'Birmingham City' to know that you are going to be in for a no-nonsense battle, and they seemed to battle better than we did that day. They were unfortunate really. We went to extra time at 1–1. I hit the post but the scoreline stayed that way for the next thirty minutes, so the game went to penalties.

I was down to take the fourth penalty. By the time it came round to me we were 3–2 up. If I scored Birmingham would be up against it. Usually I will try to place a penalty. On this occasion I think I got a bit too excited and I decided to hit it as hard as I possibly could. I smashed it against the keeper. I was in danger of looking like an idiot as Birmingham pulled level with their next kick. After the five penalties it was 4–4 and it was down to me not converting my spot kick.

Carra, the defender, stepped up for the sixth and scored, while Andy Johnson, the Birmingham striker, failed. It was a first trophy for Houllier and a big one for us because we felt we were at the start of something.

It *was* the start of something. In 2003 we were back in Cardiff, this time to face Manchester United. This was an odd one for me. Houllier had decided to play the youngsters in the team in the earlier rounds of the competition and before the final I hadn't played a single game in the League Cup.

Having got to the final though, the manager was taking

no chances and he wanted to put out his strongest side. We played well against United and were managing to hold on to a 1–0 lead when I threaded a ball through to Michael Owen who wrapped the game up at 2–0.

Obviously we were delighted to win, but as I sat in the dressing room and looked at my medal I began to feel that things were a bit unfair. I went over to Thommo with my medal. 'Hey Thommo,' I said, 'here's my medal. Give it to one of the kids. They got us here. They deserve the medal more than me.'

Thommo waved his hands up and down in the way that Scousers do. It's as if they are trying to establish their balance on a wobbly skateboard, and when accompanied by a lilting tone in the voice, it's a gesture that's intended to be calming and conciliatory. He almost sounded a little hurt as he said, 'Or eey. No yer don't Didi. Yer havin dat medal. I'll get some more done for da kids. Yer sound.'

Thommo was sound too. He arranged to get more medals and I kept mine. Yet it was a gesture that I meant sincerely. Being part of the team and valuing everyone who had made an effort for us was more important to me than personal glorification.

Looking at 2002 it was definitely the year of the crash. We qualified for the Champions League 2002/03 competition and we went into the group stage in the autumn of 2002. We were heading for another crash and this time, in a subtle way, it was to have a monumental impact upon the history of Liverpool Football Club.

You would have thought that with a group stage involving Basel, Spartak Moscow and Valencia we would have a reasonable chance of progressing. Now I've played football all of my life, all over the world and against the best of the best. When we crashed out of the Champions League in the group stage it was largely because we suffered twice at the hands of the best team I have ever played against. I'm pretty clear on this. Not the most famous or glamorous name in world football, nor the most decorated, but the Valencia team of 2002 were superbly organised and possessed an amazing player in the Argentine Pablo Aimar.

When we played them at Mestalla we were completely outclassed. Not just beaten but totally outclassed. We had three shots on target all night. We were lucky to come away with only a 2–0 defeat. Then they came to Anfield and they did exactly the same as they did at their place. We couldn't get the ball from them and when we did, through frustration we were trying to play the ball in dangerous areas. They did us again, this time 1–0. I've played in games when I've lost 4–0 and come off the pitch feeling better than I did that night. It was horrible, yet if you stood back and looked at what they did to us, you had to say 'respect'.

I couldn't help but admire this team and the way they had been set up. As we walked off the pitch downhearted and defeated I looked over to the celebrating bench of the Valencia team. A big huddle had formed as they bounced up and down, wrapped up in their celebratory joy. As the huddle unfolded and the players ran over to applaud their fans, there stood a man who had been in the centre of the group. He was small and smiling, with a receding hairline. He was taking in the atmosphere with the air of a man who felt he had a right to stand proudly in such a famous arena.

His name was Rafael Benitez. At that time not many had heard of him, yet I think on that night a few people that mattered in the higher echelons of Liverpool Football Club had noticed him. During a night of disappointment for us, the small, smiling man with the receding hairline had become a small, smiling blip on the radar screen of Liverpool FC.

It was a small blip that was going to shake the world.

CHAPTER FIVE

FROM WACKER TO WACKER

'In which Herr Didi turns to God in an attempt to avoid becoming Private Hamann'

Here's a pub quiz question for you. Which Liverpool player started off as a Wacker before becoming a Wacker?

You may have already guessed that it was me. It may sound like a clue to a cryptic crossword, but it's true. I started out a Wacker and found my spiritual home as . . . a Wacker.

I actually started my career at the lesser-known end of the Munich footballing spectrum – Wacker Muenchen. I began playing as an amateur in the early days under the tutelage of my dad, who was a pretty decent coach. I like the idea that my career peaked *and* I found my spiritual home in the land of the Wackers. Way back in the early days of the Liverpool docks, the Wacker had an important function. He was given the daily provisions to keep a group of men from going hungry during a long day's physical toil. Each portion of food given out was called a 'wack', and even today you will hear people like the Cultural Attaché for Bootle saying things like 'Eh you've had your wack'. For a long time, even in recent history, Scousers have also been known as Wackers.

So that's the cryptic crossword over with. I just like the idea that without even realising it my career took me from being a Wacker to being a Wacker. That's a kind of poetic, romantic turn of events, which I like because I look at my relationship with Liverpool as a magnificent romance.

It was my dad that started me on football. He had to do something good because being a senior policeman he was what's known in Liverpool as a 'bizzy'. That would have been bad enough, but his special area was speeding fines and parking tickets. You can imagine he was hardly the most popular man in Munich. Seriously though, he was a fantastic dad and when he was not working he spent pretty much all of his time coaching the local youth teams at Wacker. He was an excellent coach and each time I moved up to a new age group Dad, as the coach, moved up with me.

The thing that Dad was obsessed with, and in retrospect I'm so glad that he was, was one- and two-touch play. He made us work on this relentlessly. Fortunately we had a group of lads that could take to it, especially the Turkish and Serbian immigrants who had great technique. So as we moved up the age groups our Wacker team was getting noticed as being skilful and ball playing. We beat the Bayern Munich youth teams a couple of times, which just didn't happen. The Bayern youth set-up was so strong that they won 10–0 every other week. It was in one of these games against Bayern that I caught the attention of a new coach that had recently joined them and I was offered the chance to sign for them as an amateur. Dad didn't really want me to make the switch, but I said that if I stayed at Wacker that he would have to move to be coach of a different age group. We had come a long way together but there is a stage when you need to come under the influence of other people. Dad put me before himself and agreed that I should move over to Bayern. Dad had done well with me because at the time I joined Bayern I was only five feet six inches. I was more Manuel than Basil Fawlty in those days. Now, as I look back, I realise that I owe everything to my brilliant dad. Little by little, day by day, he laid down a foundation that would stand me in good stead for the future.

I've no idea what Mum was putting in the sauerkraut at that time, but I rocketed a whole nine inches between the ages of sixteen and eighteen, which was a pretty miraculous growth spurt. I was now beginning to look something like a footballer, but I think for a time in those early days at Bayern I was still five feet six inches inside. I might have been walking around in the frame of a man, but confidence-wise I wasn't there yet.

It was a massive move to go from Wacker to Bayern. Imagine it. Bayern were my team, they were already European legends having won the European Cup three years in succession during the 1970s and when we played we didn't just play in any old stadium. We played in the Olympic Stadium, the centrepiece of the 1972 Olympics. That was pretty special.

It was a pretty intimidating experience for a young man. The senior players didn't welcome me as I had expected that they might. It was as if they looked at the young players with a mixture of fear and suspicion . . . as though you may one day edge them out of the team and then take their place, which was strange because I was just a kid trying to find my feet.

I'll never forget how that made me feel. I was a little disillusioned that the older players were not interested in helping to bring young talent through. I found it quite unnerving, and ever since I made a breakthrough I've always made it my business to go out of my way to help the young lads who are just starting out. They don't always want to listen to me, but I've always tried to help them because my early Bayern experience left such a mark on me.

The senior players might not have wanted to see anything in me, but I had the good fortune to have a legend as a manager. The great Franz Beckenbauer – the original Kaiser – saw something in me. So I started to think, 'Well if he can see something in me, I must be all right.' However, building the confidence and the belief that I had a right to be there was a slow process.

Beckenbauer phased me into the Bayern Munich first team, which for a Munich boy was a dream come true. I should have been on cloud nine but I didn't feel that way because I didn't really feel as if I was accepted. Then one day I got a serious wake-up call. My mum asked me to go down to the cellar to get something. The next thing I knew I was having some kind of a fit. I was lying on the cellar floor helpless. I had had a transient ischemic attack, and apparently they're not that uncommon and can just happen without warning. It's a kind of mini-stroke. My wife at the time, Tina, came and found me on the floor and got me to hospital. For a time I was paralysed down one side of my body. I'm sure that lots of my colleagues who have grown used to my measured approach to training never thought that they would see the words 'fit' and 'Didi Hamann' written in the same sentence.

This was quite a shock to the system. I hadn't really grasped the possibilities of being a professional footballer yet, and for a moment I thought it might have been taken away from me. I was concentrating too much on the things that were making me feel uncomfortable and not enough upon the incredible opportunity that lay in front of me. With my recovery complete, I was now going to try to establish myself as a regular first-team player and more importantly I was determined that I was going to enjoy it.

There are moments in your life that are turning points, whether it's your day-to-day life or your football life. Do footballers have moments when they suddenly realise they can make it? I certainly did. In truth, when I first got into the team at Bayern I was not really ready, physically or mentally. I still felt intimidated by the older players and I didn't really feel as though I was a proper part of things.

Even though I was in the same team as amazing players such as Oliver Kahn, Christian Ziege, Markus Babbel, Mehmet Scholl, Jurgen Klinsmann, Lothar Matthaus and Jean-Pierre Papin, I just didn't see myself as being in their league. I should have really. Anyone that gets their name on the same team-sheet as those guys should feel pretty made up. Yet I didn't feel like I should have been there. But with players like that around good things inevitably happen and we made it to the

1996 UEFA Cup final against Bordeaux, which was a two-legged tie. This was a pretty amazing thing for a twenty-two year old, but it doesn't always register with you when you are young.

The first leg was at our own Olympic Stadium and we won comfortably 2–0. In the second leg at the Stade du Parc Lescure in Bordeaux, I felt I was having a really good game and was enjoying it as we went 2–0 up on the night and 4–0 up on aggregate. I felt relaxed and comfortable, partly due to the comfortable lead we had built up. Then I had a remarkable realisation as I looked around and began to soak up the situation as we had eased the pressure on ourselves with a commanding lead. For the first time really, I felt that I belonged in this sort of arena. As I looked up it suddenly dawned on me that I was playing against Zinedine Zidane, who was on his way to being ranked as the greatest player on the planet three times. Also on the field were Christophe Dugarry and Bixente Lizarazu, who just two years later would be World Cup winners along with Zidane. Not just that, but I was playing well and felt totally at ease in this illustrious company. It was as if a light bulb had switched on in my head. From that moment I felt mentally, physically and emotionally ready. I was going to be a successful footballer regardless of the thoughts of the senior players.

One of the big differences in playing for a German club and an English club is the dressing-room culture. In England, at times it felt like you were in an underground nightclub as you entered the changing rooms, with music thumping all over the place and players reacting to the beat. Because of the music, anyone wanting to have a conversation would have to talk louder and so the whole volume of everything lifted.

By contrast, going into a German dressing room was more like walking into a reading room at the British Library. It was always very quiet and that's the way I prefer it. German players tended to talk to each other or just find a quiet space and prepare themselves for the game. The blaring music seems to be largely an English phenomenon and in truth I think it is a big distraction. I was glad when music was banned for a time while I was at Liverpool.

The other big difference in the dressing room in Germany was what tended to happen after a game. German players are a lot more open to having a go at each other about things that happened in a game as soon as the game is over and right there in front of everyone. In particular at Bayern, where there was always a European XI on the park, we had a whole team of players with very strong opinions and they were not afraid to voice them. It happened especially when Giovanni Trapattoni was our manager, because although he was a brilliant manager his grasp of German was not good enough to enable him to say anything off the cuff. Jurgen Klinsmann and Lothar Matthaus in particular would tend to get stuck into players verbally. It didn't escalate beyond that, but I think often they did it because Trapattoni couldn't.

Strangely enough, with all the pressure of the Premier League and the massive amounts of testosterone flying around, with the exception of Phil Thompson, I rarely saw this happen in England and I think it's much better that way.

It was also noticeable that in England the press officer has a lot of power. We were in big trouble if we ever spoke to a journalist without it first being sanctioned by the press officer. In Germany things are a bit more chaotic and players tend to have links and allegiances to particular newspapers. Lothar Matthaus was known to be the favourite son of the *Bild* newspaper and a lot of things that would never be allowed in England got printed there and in rival papers that used other players as their sources. Players would be critical of each other in the press and sometimes even openly critical of the manager and though this caused occasional fallings-out and chaos in the dressing room, it just seemed to go on unchecked.

The Germans have also got themselves into a bit of a mess over public access to training. When I was at Bayern all training sessions were open to the public, and it's not unusual during the school holidays to have five or six thousand people at a training session. Of course this has been the way for many years and they are finding it difficult to change. There is a club shop at the training ground and on a good day they might bring in £100,000 just for letting people in. So it has become a vital part of the German football business model that seems difficult to alter.

When I came to England I was really pleased to find that training sessions were private affairs firmly behind closed doors. I think this is right. We are working, and you wouldn't walk into someone's office while they were going about their work. The presence of fans at training makes players behave differently. Sometimes they will avoid saying something that needs to be said because they are under scrutiny, and I think it takes something away from what you can achieve in training. Trapattoni managed to get one session a week held in private; I would prefer to see it the other way around. I don't want to cut the fans out, but I think it's more reasonable to do one or two open sessions a year. The rest of the time the players should be focusing on their work and nothing else.

Of course the legendary German efficiency was a major difference too. Some people think that this is something of a myth, but I can assure you it isn't. From a very early age we are immersed in a culture that values orderliness, tidiness and control. You only have to walk through a German city to see it with your own eyes. The streets are clean and well maintained, people keep their cars clean and their houses tend to be pristine.

Inevitably this attitude seeps into everything that we do. Today, Premier League clubs look after their players like prized assets, but we were doing that in Germany years ago, and nobody does it better than Bayern Munich. If a player has a problem of any kind, professional or personal, it will be sorted out with one phone call.

At Bayern we did something that I haven't seen any other club do. When we played in European competitions we always arrived in our own beautifully polished and valeted coach. If we were playing in Moscow, a journey of over 1,200 miles, the team would fly but the moment we stepped out of the airport our own Bayern Munich-emblazoned coach would be sitting there waiting for us. It had left three days earlier and arrived with precision timing. Everything at Munich happened like clockwork.

We were conditioned to believe that to come second was not acceptable and that winning was the goal. But you don't win a league or a cup by winning one game or a couple of games, you have to be consistent. I think Germans have a more strategic, long-term view. They are not as unemotional as they are portrayed, but they tend to remain level-headed until the long-term goal is achieved. Then you will be in no doubt about the ability of Germans to show emotion. When the time is right, they can party with the best of them and if there was a partying World Cup the Germans would do as well as they do on the football pitch.

Part of our disciplined approach of course comes from the fact that all young people have to do a period of national service. I was aware of this as I turned eighteen and I didn't really want to do it because I was beginning to make progress at Bayern and I was concerned that a spell in the army would slow me down.

I'd been told that one way of getting around national service was to be registered as a student. So I thought that if I could get on to some kind of course, by the time it was over I might be getting to an age where the national service draft system would pass me over for a younger model. So I headed down to the university on admissions day to see if I could sort something out. When I arrived the large hall was crammed with excited would-be students all lining up to register for their chosen course. I had no intention of taking the course; I just needed to be a registered student to avoid the army, so the sooner I could get out of there the better.

I asked for advice from a woman who seemed to be organising things. 'What is going on here?'

There was a series of long queues and she began pointing at each line. 'Here we have the line for economics.' I looked and there must have been a hundred people moving forwards at a snail's pace. She waved towards another line. 'And here we have the line for psychology.' Again, there was a massive queue going nowhere. Whirling around, she gestured towards a third line. 'Then there is the line for theology.' I looked at this line and there were only about four people there. Theology obviously wasn't a very popular subject, but it had got my attention. The woman was being really helpful.

'Have you thought about which subject you might want to take?' she asked.

'Yes,' I replied, 'I've always been fascinated by theology.'

At that moment I thanked God for theology.

I went and stood in the short theology queue and within five minutes I was a bona fide, card-carrying, registered theology student. I never actually went to a single class but my student card kept the army off my back. Also, I later realised that I had stumbled upon a tremendous chat-up line that I could use at parties. 'Yes, I'm studying theology,' I'd say with a studious glint in my eye. They must have imagined that I was both intelligent and God-fearing. Girls must have thought that I seemed like a safe pair of hands. Round about midnight, they usually found out that I was.

My theology course kept me on the register for one semester, which in Germany is about six months. With my non-existent attendance record I could hardly go back and register for another course so I just had to hope that with the passing of time the army had forgotten all about me.

Even though I was beginning to break into the team at Bayern I still lived at home with Mum and Dad and slept in the same bedroom that I had as a little boy. Mum brought in the post one morning and handed a letter to me across the breakfast table. It looked official and important. I opened it. It said, 'Dietmar Hamann: You are instructed to attend the Munich army barracks to commence your National Service.'

Damn. I thought that my student ruse had been enough for me to get overlooked. I had no option, I just had to go and get it over with. There were only two other ways out. There was a provision in the law that because of the Nazi persecution of Jews and homosexuals, these groups could claim an exemption and opt out of national service. I checked myself out in the mirror and decided that I couldn't bluff my way through by claiming to be Jewish and I wasn't even going to try the homosexual route, so that was it. I had to go and serve my country.

Private Hamann duly reported for duty. I picked up my grey German Army uniform, a pair of hobnail boots and a rifle. It was a pretty tough life, we did a lot of square bashing, we went on long marches and we cleaned things, in particular the rifle. The funny thing was that despite all the training we were never allowed to fire that rifle. If we had ever been involved in active service I guess we would have had to wear the enemy down with demonstrations of our marching and cleaning skills.

The army were very good with me though. They knew that I was breaking through into the team at Bayern so they allowed me to go to training in the evenings. So I had quite a long and physical day all in all. We rose at 6 a.m. and then spent a full day marching or whatever it was we were doing, and would knock off at 5 p.m. The other lads would head back to the barracks for some rest and relaxation, meanwhile I had to get myself across to the Bayern training ground. It had been arranged that I could train with the second team, which trained in the evenings. I had to get my training done and get myself back to the barracks before the 10.30 p.m. curfew that I had been given. I did that five days a week. When you think of it, those were long, hard days – sixteen and a half hours a day and playing football as well.

A routine like that teaches you a thing or two about yourself and there's no doubt that it definitely instils some hard-core discipline, which is as essential in life as it is in football. If you can get through a day like that, then when you resume your normal life everything seems easier.

At first, I hated the idea of doing national service but I'm so glad that I did it. That discipline, together with the Bayern Munich attitude that coming second isn't good enough, probably did a lot more to put me in the amazing situations I've found myself in than I sometimes realise.

My one regret is that I never did get to shoot that rifle, but shooting was something that I'd be doing a lot more of in foreign fields in the years to come.

CHAPTER SIX

RAFA'S RED REVOLUTION

'Rafa takes away Didi's right to a single room
in the name of male bonding'

Where were you when it happened? For Liverpool fans and players, the day that Gerard Houllier got taken ill is our JFK moment. They say that everyone who was alive when US president John F. Kennedy was shot dead remembers exactly where they were when they heard the news.

For us it is the same with regards to Gerard's heart attack.

I was as loyal as anyone to Gerard. He was the one who brought me in from Newcastle and he had made me an integral part of a very successful team that still hadn't reached its full potential. We had won the UEFA Cup, the UEFA Super Cup, the FA Cup, two League Cups and the FA Community Shield. Gerard had put Liverpool back on the trophy-winning map just in the nick of time and nobody should ever forget what he did.

The home game against Leeds United on 13 October 2001 was an early kick-off on account of the passionate rivalry between the two sets of fans. I was suspended for the game having reached my disciplinary points quota, and I sat in the stands next to Michael Owen. At half-time we were 1–0 down to a Harry Kewell goal. Michael and I stayed in our seats during the break and Michael's mobile rang and he answered. As the call went on he began to look concerned. 'That was my mate,' he said. 'He's watching Sky and it's just come on the telly that Gerard is ill.' At that stage we didn't know if it was flu or food poisoning, though sure enough Gerard didn't emerge for the second half and slowly details began to emerge.

Through word of mouth and phone-call updates from people who had access to Sky Sports, details about just how serious the situation was unfolded. After the game, the lads who had played said that he was giving the team talk when he stopped and said 'I'm not feeling very well' and he walked out into the corridor. It was there that he suffered a major heart attack and he was then rushed to hospital.

It seems that Gerard's life was saved by the intervention of the brilliant doctors that treated him. He went in with a 10 per cent chance of survival and somehow survived eleven hours of open-heart surgery. I found this a very worrying and scary time. We went to the hospital in small groups to see him but it was difficult to do anything other than offer moral support.

Phil Thompson took over the running of the team and was absolutely brilliant. Thommo somehow managed to curb his 'bull in a china shop' behaviour and was calmer and more measured. I don't know if it was due to the extra responsibility or perhaps seeing what had happened to Gerard may have given him something of a reality check. Whatever it was, Thommo should always be remembered for that period when he showed true leadership qualities and did a fantastic job for the club.

Some months later Gerard was able to come to the training ground to visit the players. It was all very emotional. He looked pale and as weak as anyone I have ever seen in my life. It was a real shock to the system. He must have dropped three or four stone. The effort of getting out to see us had clearly taken its toll and he looked very tired but he was determined that he would address us as a group. His voice was quiet and weak as he said, 'You are doing very well. You must keep it up. I'm watching your every move, so don't think that anything goes unnoticed.' He then gave a cheeky grin. It was clear that even though he had come very close to death and he was very frail, he was thinking about his team all of the time.

Gradually, as he grew stronger, he started to come back into the club, a day here, a couple of days there, until he was back to his full-time role. Incredibly the Gerard Houllier that had been taken away from us was back, and he was just as ambitious and just as full of dreams about the future.

After a period of trophy-winning success, Gerard made a few signings that didn't really work out, such as El-Hadji Diouf, Salif Diao and Bruno Cheyrou. Nicolas Anelka's loan move wasn't made permanent and fans became disgruntled, believing that he had failed to adequately replace Gary McAllister and Jari Litmanen. On 24 May 2004 it was announced in a press conference that Gerard would be leaving Liverpool by mutual consent. At the press conference to announce his departure he said, 'If Liverpool want to go back to the seventies and eighties they can, but not with me.'

It seemed like an inappropriate time for Carra and I to suggest we have a farewell drink at Flares nightclub.

With Gerard gone, I watched the managerial situation with interest from the German international base in Portugal where we were about to go crashing out of EURO 2004.

When the man to replace Gerard was under discussion, there must have been those in the Anfield boardroom who, like me, had remembered the intelligent way that Valencia had beaten us over two legs in the Champions League in 2002. If there had to be a successor to Gerard, then someone who understood the European game and had made a mark on it was the order of the day. The smiling little man with the receding hairline who celebrated on the Anfield touchline had won two Spanish titles and a UEFA Cup in just three years with Valencia. When I heard that the Liverpool board had decided to appoint Rafael Benitez I was intrigued.

I had been mightily impressed with the way his team had played against us. It was clever and incisive. Over the two games it felt like a performance that was masterminded. Benitez had been the mastermind.

I wondered what I could learn from this man.

I returned to the club a little later than the others because of international duty. My first recollection of Rafa was as I was walking down the corridor at the training ground. He was coming in my direction and he stopped me and welcomed me back. He beckoned me towards the gym and we sat down on a bench in between pieces of equipment.

'Do you want to stay here?' he said.

I said enthusiastically, 'Yes. I really want to stay here.' I wanted him to be in no doubt about where I wanted to be.

'Good,' he replied. Then he looked at me quizzically for a moment. 'They tell me that you smoke.'

What could I say? I suppose I could have promised to give up or denied it or said it was an exaggeration. Instead, I calmly looked back into his eyes and politely said, 'Yes. That's right. Sometimes more, sometimes less, but yes I do.'

I have no idea what he was expecting me to say. Maybe I surprised him by just being honest. He took it in for a moment and then simply said 'Oh'. The conversation was over. He got up and went about his business.

It was a simple and brisk exchange and, although I didn't realise it at the time, I had just met a footballing genius.

At first Rafa had a philosophy of creating a very tight-knit group. He only had a small team around him, so when we went on a preseason tour to the USA all of us were able to fit on to quite a small private jet. I don't know why, but for some reason we were given the use of the Miami Heat team's private jet and it must have had only about thirty seats.

There was Rafa, his assistant Pako Ayestaran, a goalkeeping coach, a doctor, a physio, a masseur and a kit man. On the playing side, we must have taken about eighteen or twenty players. Compared to some tours these days, which involve massive backroom teams and huge squads, this was like a small family trip to the seaside.

As it was only a small jet we had to stop twice to refuel, in Greenland and in Newfoundland, before making our way to Boston. We had a couple of friendly games to play and we were going to do our preseason training in New Jersey. This was a good opportunity to see what Rafa had in his managerial locker.

I can see now that Benitez came into the club and tried to do two things. One – he wanted to lift the club out of what he saw as its complacency and two – to build the team spirit.

From day one I rated him very highly. I thought that everything he said was spot on and I believed that with this guy we would have every chance of building upon the foundation that Gerard Houllier had laid. Not everyone in the squad felt the same as I did. In the early training sessions Rafa was very much into the detail. He spent a lot of time on team shape and we would do little exercises so that everyone knew where they were supposed to be and what they were supposed to do given different scenarios. Of course you can't just practise these things once, you have to do them over and over until they become hard-wired and people respond to the picture they are seeing on the pitch without consciously thinking.

This got to some of the lads, because if it took an hour or two hours, Rafa would stick at it until he was satisfied. There was a bit of moaning going on in the changing room.

'The training's shit,' said one.

'It's really boring,' said another.

I wasn't going to listen to this. It's not like me to be confrontational but I felt that I just had to speak out. I said, 'Shut up. Listen, I'm telling you this guy is different class. All of this is going to make you better players. You mark my words. Now shut it.' I think a few of the lads were taken aback by this but I'd played under a lot more managers than the young lads and felt that I was in a better position to judge what was going on.

It's true that there was a lot of repetition and, yes, sometimes it was a bit boring. However, this was the way that Giovanni Trapattoni had worked when I was at Bayern Munich and I had seen what a difference that this attention to detail can make. Some of the lads just wanted to play five-a-side all of the time. I said, 'That's OK if you are happy with finishing twelfth in the league. I'm not, and this guy is going to take us to another place. You've got to believe me when I say that this guy is special.'

Rafa started his quiet revolution with some really simple things. He spent time observing the way we were with each other. First, he broke down the cliques. He said, 'I've been watching you all. The French are over here, the Spanish are in this corner and the English are in another corner.' I guess that I was regarded as one of the English because he didn't mention the Germans. He continued, 'I'm not happy with the way that you are all separate. You are a team and you must do things together. When you have dinner together from now on, nobody leaves the table until everyone has finished. I've seen people getting up and going to their rooms before others have even started their soup. That stops now. You will all communicate with each other and show respect for each other.' I liked that approach. It made a lot of sense to me and I was on board right away.

One of the things I had agreed with Gerard Houllier when I first came to Liverpool was that I was always to have a single room when we were staying away. That wasn't me acting like a prima donna. I just liked my own space and I liked to get myself mentally ready for a game, which I felt that I could do better in solitude. Gerard had accepted this and so I always roomed alone apart from in exceptional circumstances when sharing was unavoidable due to us taking an extra-large squad or something like that.

My single room was something that I had to sacrifice when Rafa took over, because he thought it was better for the team to break our normal patterns of doing things. He gave out his instructions. 'We are not having regular room-mates from now on. I will decide who rooms with who.' In a roundabout way this meant that I would be rooming with *someone*, whoever it was that Rafa thought I should be with. I decided that I would just have to swallow it. If he believed that this was one of the things that would make us into a better team then I wanted to go along with it.

Rafa changed the rooming schedule on a regular basis so that players didn't become insular and so that more wide-spread relationships could begin to form. After a while though, it began to settle down and we noticed something of a pattern emerge. He tended to like to put the two centre backs together; he would put the left fullback with the left winger; the right fullback with the right winger; two midfield players would room together; and so on. So, although Rafa never announced his team until an hour or so before the kick-off, we realised that nine times out of ten the rooming rota would reveal the teamsheet. Either that or he read out the rooming schedule thinking he was reading out the team-sheet.

Having done something to change the relationships within the group, the second big thing that I think he did was much more incisive. He called a meeting and unceremoniously issued a challenge to the players' pride.

With everybody present he calmed the room and looked around with a grave expression on his face. He was serious in the way that he took the players on.

'How many points were you behind Arsenal last season?' he demanded.

It was hardly a *Mastermind*-type question but the response was quite amazing.

After an awkward silence somebody shouted, 'Eeer, twenty-six?'

Then a French voice was sure that it was twenty-eight.

Another voice piped up, 'No, no, it was twenty-nine.'

The room erupted in a hubbub of discussion as players began to agree and disagree with each other. Benitez called a halt to it. 'Stop. Stop talking.' When he had everyone's undivided attention he took a little pause and said, 'I will tell you. You were thirty points behind Arsenal. Do you believe that you are thirty points worse than Arsenal?'

This time there was not an awkward silence. The room sounded like the London Stock Exchange during a bull market as all at once the players seemed to want to take on anyone who thought that we were thirty points worse than Arsenal. Yet it was there in black and white. Arsenal had exceeded our points tally by a massive margin. It was clear from the vague answers about the size of the margin that Liverpool had stopped comparing themselves with the best. Benitez realised that he had got a reaction.

He waited again for calm in the room. He had made his point. 'Let's go to work,' he said. He stormed out of the room like a little matador that had just dispatched a feisty bull. Everyone's eyes followed him. Any remaining complacency would not remain for long with this manager in charge.

If you look closely, you can spot the characteristics of Rafa's teams. He has what I call 'handwriting' that he imposes on his sides. The handwriting he had applied at the brilliantly organised Valencia was the handwriting that he was trying to impose upon our Liverpool side. Organisation, closing down and passing were all Rafa hallmarks. If managers start to change their handwriting then they didn't really believe in it in the first place. Rafa believed in his style and approach.

It was an approach that began to be laid down in training. I realised how meticulous it was when it was getting close to my dad's fifty-eighth birthday. I went to see Pako, the assistant manager. 'Pako,' I said, 'it's my dad's birthday in four weeks' time and I'd like to go over to Munich to see him. Will I be able to go?'

Pako pulled out a large book and opened it. Inside, the whole of the next six weeks was programmed, minute by minute, hour by hour. It was a programme that we would stick to, win, lose or draw. He looked up the day I wanted to go and said, 'We are doing some physiological tests on that day, but if you come in and do them the day before, I will let you go.' Pako made a small exception to the rules.

In all the time that I worked under Rafa the training never once changed from the schedule that was laid down in Pako's book, because Rafa believed in what he was doing. He was not one of those managers that would impose a double training session if we lost a game. If things weren't working he would look at changing the team not the training regime and philosophy. I think it's a very important thing for a manager to have an unshakable belief in an underlying philosophy. Change things by all means but if you don't have a strong foundation that you believe in, then changes will take you all over the place.

In Germany it happened a lot that managers imposed a double training session because results were not going the right way. To me this seemed to be more for the benefit of the fans and the media, to try to show that the players were being punished. I don't think it is a good thing to do. Firstly, the players have got an excuse for not trying too hard because they are saving themselves for a double session. Secondly, the manager is showing doubt about the validity of what he asked you to do a week earlier.

There was no such doubt when it came to Rafa's approach. We followed Rafa's handwriting and Pako's book whatever happened. Win, lose or draw.

For those who weren't as keen on Rafa's training regime and those that may have doubted his ability, our first Premier League campaign under his management, taken on its own, gave them plenty to crow about. It was erratic. We had good periods followed by unexpected defeats and some bad spells. All in all, even though Rafa had chastised us for finishing thirty points behind Arsenal the year before he arrived, by the end of his first season we were even further off the pace. We ended up thirty-seven points behind the champions Chelsea.

For me, this wasn't the disaster that it first appeared. This was just Rafa going through a learning curve. He was looking at what he had available to try to establish his handwriting on the team. While he was busy imposing his system, tinkering here and there, he was also actively looking for players who could help him to implement his style.

Whereas Gerard Houllier had built a cadre of fellow countrymen, it seemed that Rafa didn't fancy too many of the French Foreign Legion. He gradually moved them out, replacing them with a group of his own fellow countrymen, the Spanish Armada, as they became known. I don't think it was a nationalistic thing, I just think he wanted a different type of player to Gerard. Of course he knew what was what in the Spanish league so it was quite natural that he should look to Spain for many of his acquisitions. He wanted players who were not simply good footballers, but who also fitted in with the handwriting that he was trying to impose upon his team.

He brought in Antonio Nunez, in part exchange for Michael Owen who went to Real Madrid; Josemi from Malaga; Xabi Alonso came from Real Sociedad; and Luis Garcia; making it four Spaniards in a row upon his arrival. He varied the pattern the following season, but still brought in other Spaniards in the form of Fernando Morientes from Real Madrid; Pepe Reina from Villarreal; Antonio Barragan of Sevilla; Miki Roque from little-known Llieda; before raiding his former club Valencia for the Argentine Mauricio Pellegrino.

This was the start of a shift away from the Houllier-type of player to the type of player that Rafa wanted. Some worked out, some didn't, but by the time Rafa left he had spent £229 million. Looking at Rafa's time in charge I can see why there was such a big turnover in players. Something like 40 per cent of his imports worked out in the long term. The 60 per cent or so that didn't work out were not bad players, it's simply that Rafa has extraordinarily high expectations. He brings people in and explains what he expects them to do, and if they don't meet his expectations that's it. They are out. An Anderson or a Nani probably wouldn't have stayed long enough to show what they could do had they joined Liverpool rather than Manchester United. In the end I think Rafa's high expectations were part of his downfall at Liverpool. There were so many players coming in with big price tags that inevitably some continuity and consistency was lost. It's extremely difficult to get a team to gel when you are changing eight, nine, ten or more players every year. Things can easily become disjointed.

Rafa had another big problem to contend with at Liverpool. Despite Houllier revamping the youth set-up and Rafa subsequently adding his twist to it, the academy wasn't producing a new Gerrard, Carragher or Fowler. The production line of young talent had almost ground to a halt as Everton became the home for talented youngsters wanting to get a chance to break through. Rooney, Rodwell and Osman were coming through while Liverpool's reputation as a buying club was becoming more entrenched.

That's still the case even today, and it presents Liverpool with a problem for the future, because this affects the perception of the parents of talented young players. If they are given a choice between Liverpool and Everton, the evidence is showing them that their lad will have a better chance of breaking into first-team football at Everton. It hurts me to say that but the facts speak for themselves.

Rafa happened to preside over a relatively barren period as far as the academy was concerned, and this together with big-ticket signings that didn't work out, saw him come under pressure.

As Rafa discovered, when you are successful there is a queue of people wanting to tell you that you are a genius, and for part of his time at Liverpool this was the case. The thing in football is that a few blips and you can go from hero to zero very quickly indeed. There are mixed opinions about Rafa on Merseyside. I've got absolutely no doubts where I stand on the matter. In the corridors and changing rooms of Anfield I met many people – the great, the talented, the legendary. I know that I only met one genius.

He was a small, smiling man with a neatly clipped beard. His name was Rafael Benitez.

CHAPTER SEVEN

ONCE A KRAUT ALWAYS A KRAUT

'Home thoughts from abroad and why England can't win when it matters'

I don't mean to be rude and I'm not trying to be provocative, but England, regardless of its undoubted talent pool, will not win another World Cup for at least a generation.

I'll explain why I think that a World Cup will be beyond the grasp of an Englishman later, but first I want to dispel the myth of the rivalry between Germany and England. The English have built up this idea that there is an intense and historic rivalry between our two countries. Obviously we've engaged in wars over the centuries and there have been some ding-dong battles on the football pitch, so there's 'a bit of previous' you might say.

Perhaps the English sense of rivalry is because its one World Cup success in 1966 came against West Germany. Since then, when it has really mattered, Germany has tended to triumph over England – even if sometimes it goes to penalties. We are less sentimental than the English. The 1966 World Cup final was an important game that we lost. That's all. We look to the future.

So for us, this rivalry doesn't really exist to the extent that I feel it does in England. If we Germans have rivalries then I would say that they would more likely be with Italy or Argentina. That's not to belittle England in any way. I think it's maybe that we have overcome the disappointment of 1966 and gone on from there, while England is still looking wistfully back to that match and to the occasions when glory has looked possible but their progress has been blocked by Germany.

So, yes, we like to beat England of course, but it is not really a big rivalry for us. Yet football has a knack of throwing up coincidences and strange turns of fate. In the 2002 World Cup qualifiers we were drawn in Group 9 with England, Finland, Greece and Albania. This was not an easy group, but we felt if we could do well against England we could qualify.

Our away fixture with England on 7 October 2000 turned out to be the last game ever at the old Wembley Stadium. After seventy-seven years the stadium that had seen so much, including the 1948 Olympic Games, the 1966 World Cup final and the famous Live Aid concert, was due to be demolished to make way for a new stadium to be built on the same site.

Of course for the English this coincidence seemed to heighten the stakes. Here was a chance to say a romantic goodbye to the country's home of football by putting one over on the perceived 'old enemy'. It couldn't have been set up better for a night of national pride. For Wembley's historic last game the England team were led by a manager who was a passionate Englishman and who had seen great success with German club Hamburg, Kevin Keegan.

The stage was set for an afternoon for the whole of England to remember, but as usual we Germans hadn't read the script. The rain lashed down as Keegan called on England to produce a performance to remember, one to hold in the memory as one of Wembley's many historic nights. The truth is though, this was a big, big game for us too. Rudi Voeller had not long since come in as manager and the German public were getting restless as we hadn't won against one of the 'big boys' of international football for two or three years. It was time for the new generation to show its true colours.

We were well up for it, but the England team seemed a little flat and short on ideas. Even in the driving rain we were able to take an early grip on the game. After thirteen minutes we got a free kick a long way out. I thought that in the difficult conditions if I could hit it quick it might just catch England out. England didn't put a wall in front of the ball as I placed it down to take the kick. Maybe they thought I was too far out to bother making an attempt on goal. Only Paul Scholes stood in the path to goal, but even he was quite a way off. I hit it quickly without any messing about. It flew in between two players on the edge of the box and dipped after about five yards. With the Wembley surface so wet it skidded off the turf. I think that Seaman, the keeper, saw it late anyway, and all he could do was get a glove to it as it went into the net. I think he should have done better really, but I'm not complaining.

Nobody realised it at the time but that was the last ever goal that would be scored at the old Wembley Stadium and it was scored by a German. The moment the final whistle went we were obviously delighted, but it was a sad way to say goodbye to Wembley as the England fans let their feelings be known with a chorus of booing directed at the England team and its manager. This was not the kind of glorious night that Keegan had envisaged. He had a reputation for not staying in positions where things didn't feel right and the moment he got to the changing rooms he announced that he was resigning as England manager.

We felt that England would be our main difficulty in the group, but we had already done the hard bit by winning against them away from home. We would see them again at our place in eleven months' time, when they would be under new management.

Because of my goal in that match I became a short-lived Internet phenomenon a few years later. As the new Wembley Stadium was being built the London Development Agency and Transport for London ran a competition to try to engage the public in this major project that was meant to epitomise sporting and national pride.

A bridge was being built to link the town centre with the new stadium, and the competition organisers invited the public to go on its website and suggest names for the new bridge. Somebody in Germany, I think, created an email with a link to the website requesting that people go to the site and suggest the name 'Hamann Bridge' and also that they should send the email to everyone in their address book. It was meant to be a comical dig at the English. The idea of

England fans having to walk across Hamann Bridge for the next hundred years must have tickled German sensibilities.

It seems that other nations were keen to have a dig at the English too, and the email began to gain traction in parts of the world where there is a traditional sporting rivalry with England. People from Scotland, Australia, Ireland, New Zealand, Wales and who knows where started to bombard this website with the suggestion of Hamann Bridge.

It must have been very irritating for the London Development Agency, whose spokesman had to admit that the most popular suggestion 'by some distance' was Hamann Bridge. However, it was ruled offside and didn't get put forward for consideration by the judging panel.

In the end the bridge was named White Horse Bridge, in honour of the horse that held back the crowd as it spilled on to the pitch during the first Wembley FA Cup final between Bolton Wanderers and West Ham in 1923.

Losing on the horses was something I'd grown accustomed to, but to lose *to* a horse, and a dead one at that, was something else.

They say that every dog has his day. Eleven months after that momentous goal at Wembley Stadium, England came to the place where I had started out with Bayern, the Olympic Stadium, Munich. It was a bit of a fortress for us, and the World Cup is something that is in the German DNA. As a nation we were pretty invincible in qualifying games. At that time we were the only country ever to have lost only one World Cup qualifier. We had played 62, won 47, drawn 14 and lost only 1.

So for any team, coming to Munich to face Germany in a World Cup qualifier was a daunting, almost thankless, task. After our win at Wembley it was not a place England would have relished coming to.

We had done well in the qualifying campaign so far and were top of the group with sixteen points from six games. England had a game in hand, but had only amassed ten points. That meant that if we could beat England in Munich then just a point from our remaining home fixture against Finland would see us through to the finals in Korea/Japan. In fact, a win would probably send us through on goal difference even if England could win their last two games.

So, this was a big night for Germany. We could practically guarantee our qualification by winning this game.

England had recovered from a hopeless position under Kevin Keegan to become our only serious challengers for qualification to the finals. It was a transformation brought about by someone who would later have a big influence on me – the Swedish 'Iceman', Sven-Goran Eriksson.

Germany's only ever defeat in a World Cup qualifier had come at the hands of Portugal in 1985, but we had already qualified by that time so perhaps some players stepped off the gas a little. Here we could deliver a hammer blow to England's hopes and take a little pressure off of ourselves.

There was quite a Liverpool contingent in the England team that night. Owen, Gerrard, Heskey and Barmby all made the starting line-up and Fowler was on the bench alongside

Liverpool old boy Steve McManaman. Not that it added any pressure. I felt we were in a good position to be able to deal with England and that when we were all back at the training ground little would be said about the game.

What actually transpired on 1 September 2001 in Munich was very un-German. Even when we were beaten we were always very hard to beat and so far during the campaign we had conceded only five goals in six games. It seemed inconceivable that England could do us serious harm that night. They are always dangerous, and you have to watch out for that, but we felt we had the upper hand.

As it turned out many considered this to be England's greatest night since 1966. We went 1–0 up quite early on. It wouldn't have been unreasonable to have expected the game to go the way that all the stats indicated, but this was not to be as the Liverpool mafia took over. Owen got an equaliser and when Deisler missed a sitter from six yards out we missed a chance to put ourselves back in the driving seat. Then Gerrard hit one into the net from thirty yards. England had their tails up and went in at half-time 2–1 up.

In the dressing room we felt hard done by; we should have been at least level at half-time. Had Deisler made it 2–1 then England might not have been able to hit back, so we were unfortunate not to be winning. We felt that the scoreline didn't truly reflect the way the game had gone, but we were not unduly concerned. It seemed like a situation that could be retrieved.

With England starting the second half carrying the momentum, and with Michael Owen on fire, we suddenly found ourselves with our backs against the wall. Michael scored another within three minutes of the restart and had completed a hat-trick after sixty-five minutes. As we pushed to try to at least recover some pride, Emile Heskey was slipped through for a one-on-one with the keeper and he calmly controlled the ball and slotted it away into the corner of the net. Germany 1 England 5. It still doesn't look right to me, but that was the scoreline being flashed across the giant Olympic Stadium scoreboard. It's an image that was so unlikely it made the front page of most English newspapers the next morning. It is now regarded as an iconic image that has become part of the folklore of English football. We took an almighty spanking for sure.

The English media celebrated yet another new dawn for the national team. Sven-Goran Eriksson and his team, who were a very strong group of players there's no doubt about that, were already being tipped for World Cup success by the British press just on the back of this one result.

But as Germans we are brought up to have an eye on the big picture. This was a disappointment for sure, but this was all about winning the World Cup and this was one qualifier out of many qualifiers. Whether we lost 1–0 or 5–1 didn't play on our minds. We lost, but we simply took the view that the group was still there to be won.

We regarded this result in the same way as we would any defeat. Nothing more, nothing less. There were no histrionics in the dressing room that night. Our manager Rudi Voeller's father had been in the crowd and had suffered a heart attack during the game and had been taken to hospital. Rudi naturally headed straight to see his father as soon as the final whistle went, so there was no detailed analysis with the manager after the match. It was another one of those occasions that puts football into perspective. Losing 5–1 is nothing compared to the possibility of losing a loved one.

Rudi returned to the team hotel while we were all having our meal; fortunately his father was doing OK. We talked a bit about the game, but it was gone and our minds turned to what we had to do next to get to the World Cup finals.

So an episode that went down in the history books of English football hardly registered in the psyche of the German players. What mattered was not the headline in the *Daily Mail* the next morning but which team could get to the World Cup finals. It was in our nature to take a strategic view of our position.

The group standings were eventually decided in the ninety-third minute of England's qualifying match against Greece at Old Trafford. England were trailing 2–1 deep into injury time. The group looked like it belonged to us, until Beckham produced another iconic moment for England fans with a fabulous free kick. There was barely time to restart the game. In due course the glut of goals that we conceded against England proved fatal. We stuttered to a 0–0 draw at home to Finland, and England's late, late draw against Greece meant that we ended up level on seventeen points each. However, England had a better goal difference than us so qualified automatically. We had to go into the play-offs and faced a tricky two-legged match against Ukraine.

It's surprising how things turn out sometimes. The trip to Ukraine had an amazing impact upon us as a group of players. We had struggled to gel after a disappointing EURO 2000 and we had been trying to find a team and a formation that would click. We weren't quite there and now we found ourselves in a freezing Kiev for a November fixture with 83,000 Ukrainians screaming for their team. This was a tough situation and we faced a tough physical side. We went 1–0 down after only eighteen minutes and then they had another good scoring chance that came back off the post. Our World Cup dreams were slipping away. As a team we really had to dig deep if we were not to face an insurmountable task in the second leg. The noise in the stadium was erupting as the Kiev crowd sensed victory, however, we managed to silence them with an invaluable equaliser. The game finished with the score at 1–1. The second leg could have gone either way.

When the Ukrainians came to Dortmund for the return fixture there was something about the camaraderie within our camp. We knew that we had been in an almighty scrap in Kiev and we had come out of it together as a team. In Dortmund, suddenly the team and the formation began to click and we ended up playing some of the best, most fluid football that Germany had played in a long, long time. Michael Ballack weighed in with two goals and the Ukrainians found themselves on the end of a 4–1 drubbing.

There was a mixture of relief and celebration when we arrived back at our hotel, but something was happening to us as a group that couldn't be described on any tactician's blackboard or in anyone's coaching manual. Coming within a game of elimination and having our collective backs against the wall had been like a team-building exercise in itself. We had become closer as a group and that closeness had shown its effect out on the pitch. There was a special atmosphere at the hotel that night. It was a legitimate time for a party, and party we did. Everybody stayed on and we eventually went to bed at seven o'clock in the morning.

Beckham's brilliant ninety-third minute free kick had given England a hero. By sending us to the Ukraine, it had given the Germans a team. We would see which team faired better when the real business began in Korea/Japan.

That run to the Korea/Japan finals was my best period as a German international. I got my first chance at international level in 1997 in a game in Dusseldorf against South Africa. We won 3–0 and I was one of the goalscorers. It was a great start for me, but the evening was a bit of an anticlimax. There were only 12,000 spectators so the ground seemed eerily empty and the atmosphere was non-existent.

This was a great time to come into the German squad. There were guys in the team who had been World Cup winners in 1990 and there was a lot that I could learn just by being in their presence. It was also a time of expectation. Just as Steven Gerrard and co. were branded England's 'Golden Generation', players like me were expected to come through and give Germany its next generation of World Cup winners.

In 1998 I was able to test myself in a World Cup finals in France. This was a great experience and was an opportunity to spend a significant amount of time working with and watching the 1990 World Cup winners that were still in the squad. I thought that being at Bayern Munich I was operating at a pretty high level, but when I was part of the training set-up with these guys it took everything to an even higher level of intensity. They weren't resting on their laurels. They were top-class professionals who had really achieved and I was beginning to see why. Just being around them, listening to them and playing against them in training was like going to the Oxford University of football.

One of the 1990 World Cup winners was Lothar Matthaus, who I knew from Bayern Munich. He had left Munich for a successful spell with Inter Milan and then come back after I had broken into the team. I always got on with Lothar and had absolutely no problems with him at all, but it seems others didn't share that view. So much so, that apparently a good proportion of the EURO 1996 squad complained to the German Football Association that they did not want to play for their country if it meant playing alongside Lothar Matthaus. If true, that's a pretty damning judgement from your teammates. I wasn't involved in that in any way, though I can see that he must have rubbed a few people up the wrong way to say the least. There was speculation about Lothar's relationship with *Bild*. The paper campaigned strongly for Lothar, especially if he wasn't in the team. Although there was no hard evidence, people jumped to the conclusion that in return for positive editorial coverage he fed titbits of news.

So in the lead-up to the 1998 World Cup in France, Lothar was not even in the reckoning for the squad and there were no thoughts of him going. This time though, in addition to the support of *Bild*, he had an excellent second half of the season with Bayern that culminated in us winning the German FA Cup. He was absolutely on fire. There was one final place in the World Cup squad that looked undecided. Mehmet Scholl was the expected choice, but Lothar's storming performances in the latter part of the season meant that he could not be ignored. This was a tricky situation for the manager, Berti Vogts. Jurgen Klinsmann was still a key player and he and Lothar didn't get on at all and some of the people that signed the letter to the German FA two years earlier were still in the squad. *Bild* did everything it could to promote the Matthaus campaign. Whether that swung it or not, nobody knows, but Scholl was out and Matthaus was in.

You can say what you like about Lothar, and people do, but you could not deny that he had something about him personality-wise. He was a bit of a charmer, to the extent that had he not been a footballer he would have been equally at home as a salesman – the type that can sell sand to the Arabs. He showed his charming salesman-like abilities big time at the 1998 World Cup and all of the players, whether they liked him or not, had to give him a pat on the back.

Our World Cup base was a beautiful hilltop hotel overlooking the Mediterranean Sea in St Paul de Vence. It was idyllic, the kind of place that you would love to take your wife or your girlfriend to. The trouble was our wives and girlfriends were staying about 20 kilometres from the hotel down in the city of Nice. The training regime was quite intense and the opportunities to be with loved ones were restricted largely by our geographical separation, which is the way manager Berti Vogts wanted it.

During our training camp the whole squad was invited to a reception at the Riviera villa owned by high-flying German businesswoman Regine Sixt. Her family started a car-rental business in Munich about a hundred years ago and she was now running it, having turned it into a global business with something like 4,000 Sixt pickup points in 100 countries. We mingled and chatted, and a common topic began to develop among some of the lads. We loved our hotel and had absolutely no complaints, it was beautiful, but it was on a hilltop out of town and there was no way to get down to see our families in Nice. Lothar was always a man who could sort things and he prided himself on his ability to use his charms to get almost anything. So players were repeatedly saying, 'Come on Lothar, see if you can get the boss to get us down to Nice for a while.'

Lothar was unruffled. 'Don't you worry, I will sort it, just be patient.'

We stayed at the reception for a couple of hours and then headed back to the hotel to get ready for another full-on training session the next day.

After a tough afternoon shift the following day, it must have been 5 p.m. when our team coach brought us back up the narrow track to St Paul de Vence. Nearing the top of the hill the coach began to slow and chug a little instead of going into the hotel parking area as usual. Someone stood up to see what was going on and let out an excited yelp. Everybody now stood up and the coach came alive with excitement as people tried to take in what was going on. The coach was unable to enter the hotel parking area because it was completely blocked. There were two car transporters crammed with Mercedes and other Mercedes beside them. There must have been twenty-five brand-new gleaming Mercedes being offloaded courtesy of Sixt. Lothar stood up triumphantly and said, 'I told you that I would get things sorted for you didn't I?' At that moment everybody loved Lothar and the silky-smooth charm that he had exuded all over Regine Sixt. Everybody, that is, except the manager Berti Vogts, who had no idea that this was going to happen.

As luck would have it we had a rest morning the following day. We just had to report in at 1 p.m. for a team meeting, a massage and any physio if we needed it, but the morning was free. As soon as dawn broke everyone was up and out faster than a German chasing the one remaining sunbed at the hotel pool. We were into the Mercs and down into Nice before Berti had even got out of bed.

Berti had his own routine that he used to share with his assistant Rainer Bonhof. Every day without fail they got up at 6.30 a.m. and went for their morning jog around St Paul de Vence before breakfast. Berti must have been expecting to see twenty-five gleaming Mercs when he went out; instead he was confronted by an empty car park. Everyone had gone to Nice.

It was a lovely morning excursion down into Nice and a great way to break up the routine of the training camp. However, when we got back for our 1 p.m. team meeting Berti didn't see it that way. He went absolutely bonkers, bouncing around the room venting his anger. 'You think you are on holiday. You are here to win the World Cup. What do you think you are doing?'

I think that he would have taken it a lot better if Lothar had let him know what was going to happen, but that was Lothar. He could certainly be charming, but his antics could provoke the most extreme reactions. One thing's for sure,

Mehmet Scholl was a good player and he would have done a good job for us, but without Lothar we would never have enjoyed our memorable mornings in Nice.

At that time the German team was very much a team in transition, trying to find a new pattern. The difficulty was that we had had such a great squad for years that it was difficult for new players to break in for a long period so our squad was not quite balanced. We had the older players with vast experience, many of whom were World Cup winners, and we had the youngsters coming through. Jens Jeremies was two months younger than me, so at twenty-four years old I was the second-youngest in the squad and Babbel and Ziege were fairly young too. So, we had the older players and the youngsters and not many players who age-wise were in the middle of these two groups. So, we were very much in a period where we were trying to create a new formula for success.

In the end 1998 was not a great World Cup for us, and it had nothing to do with Lothar's Mercedes stunt. We were a team assimilating new young blood and we crashed out in the quarter-finals being well beaten by Croatia 3–0. I missed an absolute sitter with my head that could have changed the game, but that's not too surprising as I only ever scored two goals with my head in all my time as a footballer.

The World Cup was followed by a poor showing in EURO 2000, where we didn't even make it through to the knockout stage. We were stuttering when it came to tournaments and the German public had high expectations. We were Germany, we had a history of doing well in tournaments. Things had to change.

When it came to the 2002 World Cup finals our defeat to

England had meant that we had to get there the hard way. Though it was a bit odd really: England qualified automatically and ended up in a tough group with Argentina, Sweden and Nigeria; meanwhile, despite our stuttering qualification, we were luckier than England, being thrown in with Saudi Arabia, Cameroon and Republic of Ireland. Cameroon were the African Champions and Ireland were always a tough nut to crack. Ours was a tricky group whereas England's was challenging to say the least.

The Saudi Arabia team had qualified for their first World Cup and they were a little in awe of the whole thing. While we were doing our warm-up they were getting their video cameras out and taking pictures of the crowd, the stadium, each other, us, anything that caught their attention. It was as if a busload of tourists had just hit town. Their heads were somewhere else, rather than on the game, which is what they should have been concentrating on.

We made sure that we got some feisty tackles in early on, and it was clear that they weren't really up for any physical stuff. They were on holiday after all. We got off to a good start against the Saudis who, although they enjoyed 47 per cent of the possession, had only one attempt on goal during the whole game. They faded in the last twenty-five minutes of the first half and conceded four goals by half-time. Having regrouped they did exactly the same in the second half, this time conceding four goals in the final twenty minutes. The game ended with an 8–0 scoreline that set us up nicely for the forthcoming games against Republic of Ireland and Cameroon.

An injury-time goal from Robbie Keane cemented a draw

for Ireland, so we had to get a win over Cameroon to be sure to go through to the knockout stage. We started well, but then we made it hard work for ourselves when Carsten Ramelow got sent off after forty minutes. However, goals from Bode and Klose saw us through a tough game that involved fourteen yellow and two red cards. On seventy-seven minutes they had a man sent off, so both teams saw out the game with ten men. We had made it through to the last sixteen.

I was benched for the 'round of sixteen' game against Paraguay, which looked certain to be heading for a 0–0 draw and extra time. With just two minutes left on the clock Oliver Neuville scored the winner. There was no time left for Paraguay to reply, so we were through to the quarter-finals, where we were to face the USA.

President Clinton held a conference call with the USA squad to tell them that he and the American nation were rooting for them in this soccerball contest. I was back in the team for this match, and it was a tough one. Something certainly had an effect on the USA team because they dominated the game. But the game's about scoring goals, and one of the great assets that we had was that if the forwards were misfiring there was every chance that Michael Ballack would pop up and score. Throughout his career he has had a happy knack not just of scoring, but of scoring goals that really matter.

That's what he did after thirty-nine minutes in this match. Before that the USA were dominant, after that the USA were dominant, but Michael's goal had sealed our place in the semi-final. A few hours earlier England had lost a 1–0 lead against Brazil and even though Ronaldinho got sent off there was no way past the remaining ten Brazilians. England went out, losing 2–1.

You had to feel for England. They had won the qualifying group, had faced the most difficult group stage and had had to overcome Denmark for the right to take on Brazil. That was a difficult route for them to try to navigate.

We meanwhile had been more fortunate and managed to come through the tough test against the USA. We were also fortunate that the tournament threw up two surprise semifinalists, Turkey and South Korea, and we were kept apart from Brazil. Turkey and South Korea were not fancied to progress to the semi-final stage, but this had been a peculiar finals. Instead of facing one of the traditional big guns of world football, we faced the more modest South Korea, while Brazil took on Turkey.

Our semi-final was a pretty even affair, but we were enjoying the better chances. The game was heading for a stalemate, when that man of ours popped up to settle it. As I said, Michael Ballack's goals tend to be significant. There are few goals more significant than the one that gets you into the World Cup final. Michael had done it again.

We had made it to the final. Even though this wasn't the best German team in recent memory, we had done the business when it mattered. You can only beat what is put in front of you and that's what we did. We had conceded only a single goal, the late effort from Robbie Keane, and we felt solid.

As expected we met Brazil in the final in Yokohama, Japan. It's a huge thing to play in a World Cup final and although Brazil are always a difficult side to play against, if you are going to win the World Cup you have to be able to beat the best.

I still think about the night of 30 June 2002, the night of the World Cup final. For many years it haunted me. I went over and over it in my mind. Should I have done things differently? Would it have changed the course of history? Even now, every so often, my mind flips back to that night and I go over things yet another time.

Every player has his own style, his own habits and his own beliefs. Sometimes the fans didn't like my philosophy but I've always protected myself as a footballer. I'd always go for a fifty-fifty ball no problems at all, but if the odds were against me I'd have no qualms in pulling back. I always wanted to be available to serve the team rather than hobbling off as a brave but bloodied gladiator and spending the next four games in the stands. It's a pragmatic and professional outlook, but as I say, sometimes the fans disapproved.

It's an outlook that I still agree with, but it was that outlook that maybe, just maybe, cost me a World Cup winners' medal. In that 2002 final against Brazil, with the game still 0–0, I got an amazing chance about eighteen yards out. The ball was crossed to me and I could not have controlled it more perfectly. In that position I would say that I would hit the target eight times out of ten and I would score four times. Here was a chance to score and put us ahead in the biggest game of them all. With the ball perfectly positioned at my feet I went to pull the trigger. As I did so I saw Lucio lunge towards me. My natural instinct to protect myself just kicked in. It was the kind of lunge that could have left you with ruptured ligaments, yet that slight split-second hesitation meant that I put the chance wide. It was a chance that I feel pretty sure that I could have put away had I not hesitated. That's not an easy thing to live with and it weighed heavily on me.

Now, with the benefit of hindsight, I can say that maybe I should have just gone for it, but at that stage we were still at 0–0. Had it been 0–1 then I feel that I would definitely have gone for it and risked injury.

That was bad enough, but I also gave the ball away in the sequence that led to the first of Brazil's two goals. Our keeper Oliver Kahn had broken his little finger, but he didn't want to come off in a World Cup final. As I gave away the ball and a Rivaldo shot came into Kahn, he did what he often did, which was palm it forward. Usually he would then collect the ball, but on this occasion he was clearly anxious about his finger and he palmed it just a little further than normal, far enough for Ronaldo to pounce. We were unable to reply and the World Cup passed us by. We were unfancied at the start of the tournament and went much further than anyone expected, but that's no consolation at all. When you grow up with a winning mentality as I had done, coming second is not enough.

I know that somewhere in a box of my belongings, probably in the attic, is a World Cup runners-up medal. It's been there since 2002 and I have never really had any desire to look at it. Most players are like that. It might sound strange, but in a way it's a healthy attitude for a professional footballer. You have got to want to be among the best and that means winning against the best in the biggest games. Nobody remembers who came second.

After the final a formal reception was held for us in Yokohama by the *bundeskanzler* (federal chancellor) Gerhard Schroeder. He was our German chancellor, the equivalent of the British prime minister. It was meant to be a celebration, but as you can imagine we weren't in the mood for a party. We had dinner and a few drinks afterwards, and people started to mingle. I was standing close to Chancellor Schroeder and I smelt the marvellous warm aroma of what can only be described as a splendid cigar. I don't think I had ever smelt a cigar quite like this one. It smelt like the nicotine equivalent of honey. I turned to look, and it was a large brown wrap that looked every bit as exquisite as it smelt. It's not every day that you play in a World Cup final, and it's not every day that you find yourself standing alongside the chancellor of your country. I turned to him and said, 'I really like your cigar. Do you have any more of those?'

He thought for a minute, perhaps mentally going through his pockets and then he said, 'No, I don't have any more with me, but I have some back at my hotel. Let me get you one.' With that he summoned his driver and sent him back to the hotel with instructions to return with a stock of these sublime cigars.

Everybody forgets just how big Japanese cities are, even Yokohama, and popping out because you've forgotten something can turn out to be a major logistical exercise. It was two hours later that the driver returned with a box of the chancellor's very special cigars. Herr Schroeder called me over and opened the box so that I could select one. He kindly lit my cigar and his own, and there we stood, chatting about this and that, bonded not by a famous World Cup victory, but by our mutual regard for the good things in life. It was worth the two-hour wait.

Later as I slept in my Yokohama hotel room I awoke in the middle of the night. The first of the action replays of my chance to put us ahead in the World Cup final began to play in my head. It was going to be a long night.

When I wore the shirt of Germany I always wore it with pride and I was fortunate enough to wear it fifty-nine times. I was a German through and through, proud and loyal to my country, yet the more time I spent in England the more I felt that there was an English dimension to me. Not that I ever let that affect my game, but it did result in me helping Steven Gerrard to acclimatise to the international scene in his first competitive game for England.

It was in EURO 2000 in Belgium/Holland. We were drawn in the same group as England. I'd heard about Stevie when I first arrived at Liverpool. People would say things like, 'Have you seen the kid that's coming through?' He was about seventeen years old and senior players would point him out to me; that's what a stir he created as he was on his way up.

When he started training with the first team I couldn't believe my eyes. I'd never seen anyone train like this. He was a total maniac. He was all over the place as if he thought he was a one-man team. You never know if a kid can make it when they first step up but you could see that this lad was a bit special. He was very raw but he had the most amazing dynamic. His problem at first was that he wanted to do everything. He wanted to defend, win the ball, bomb forward, cross, score a couple, pour the tea at half-time, wash the cups, score a couple more after the break as well, clean the changing rooms and drive the team bus.

That's a great attitude to have, but although you might be able to play in overdrive like he did for a game or two, you can't keep it up over a long season. I always remembered the feeling of inadequacy I had at Bayern Munich and the lack of interest shown in me by the senior players, so I made it my business to try to help Stevie and guide him a little. He had all the talent and all the energy, but if he couldn't be more discerning about when and when not to use it I could see him burning himself out very quickly. He also had a degree of recklessness. His intensely competitive nature and his physical attributes sometimes saw him go for things that he shouldn't have done. He could turn a game in a moment or get sent off, depending on how the referee saw it.

So I started to talk to Stevie both in training and during games. I gave him little pieces of advice about positioning and self-control. In doing this I saw his best attribute shine through. The difference I noticed between Stevie and a lot of other young players was that he listened and he learned very quickly. If you told him something he got it right away and there was no need to tell him twice. With all of his natural attributes he was always going to be a good player. By listening and thinking about things he has turned into a great player.

When I first started playing with Stevie it was not uncommon for him to lose his position in a game maybe twenty times. Within a year it was more like fifteen and then after that you would be hard pushed to see him lose position even five times in a game. He improved his game year on year because of his great dedication and willingness to take advice and act upon it.

I'd grown accustomed to talking Stevie through situations and he was a good mate as well. On 17 June 2000 England and Germany met at EURO 2000 in the Belgian city of Charleroi. Both teams needed a win. We had drawn our first game against Romania, while England had lost against Portugal. There was no room for error for either side if we were to have a chance of going through. As we came out of the tunnel at the Stade du Pays de Charleroi he caught my eye and winked and I gave him an encouraging nod.

He was on the substitutes' bench. I went over and said, 'Is there any chance of you coming on?' He had only just turned twenty so he was still untried at this level and he seemed to think he was taken there to adjust to the England international scene.

'No chance,' he replied.

It was just a natural thing for me to take an interest in Stevie and his progress because it was what I had been doing ever since I met him.

It was a hard-fought game from the start, as you would expect. I had a couple of chances in the first half; one that I hit too close to David Seaman and he took it comfortably, and another that went just wide. England posed a threat too, with Scholes having an effort cleared off the line.

The pace increased in the second half and after fifty-three minutes Beckham arced in a free kick that Michael Owen misjudged. This left the ball to fall kindly for the England captain Alan Shearer. He headed past Oliver Kahn to put England one up.

It was a blow but there was still time to pull it back. We began to step up a gear and you had the feeling that we could come back. After an hour, the England manager Kevin Keegan surprised Stevie by bringing him on for his competitive debut. He replaced Michael Owen, which gave the impression that England were going to try to dig in and see the game out.

I could see that Stevie was a bit nervous as he tried to fit into the game, and it just seemed to me to be the natural thing to do to talk him through it. As I ran past him I said, 'Stevie, just keep doing what you are doing, you're doing all right.'

There was a pause in the play and he came over and said, 'I'm shitting myself.'

I suppose I could have taken advantage of his fragile state, but this was my mate and this was a big break for him, it was the start of his international career. Instead I said, 'Just relax and do what you normally do. If you do that you are going to be fine.'

Ever since I'd first met him I'd always said that you only have to tell him things once. After I told him to relax he just seemed to do exactly that and he settled into his normal all-action combative mode. We were beginning to impose ourselves, and I whipped the ball past Stevie and headed towards the England goal. That shocked him because he had never seen me do anything like that in training, but he should have known I saved myself for the games. Training tricks I left to other people. The next thing I knew, he had clattered me unceremoniously. As I went down I let out a shriek to make sure that the referee registered that this was a foul and hopefully to get him to put the brakes on Stevie imposing his physical presence.

You might have thought that Stevie would have been a bit grateful for my reassuring words, but he had moved on quickly from being a nervous rookie international to being his normal, intensely competitive self. He turned and stood over me screaming at me to get up. 'Come on Didi, if you don't get up I'll get a yellow. Two yellows and I miss the quarter-finals.' He obviously hadn't done his homework in the way that Phil Thompson would have done when he played against Germany, because when I swore at him in German he just looked blank.

England were 1–0 winners, their first competitive victory against us since 1966. Stevie had made it through his first competitive international and was on his way to eventually captaining his country. He later told the press that when he brought me down I 'screamed like a girl'. He showed his naivety there. I'd already given Stevie quite enough assistance for one game, and in fact I screamed like a man who was trying to get another man into trouble. I wasn't even hurt – sometimes you just have to 'play the game'.

Stevie was my midfield partner at Liverpool and I found it interesting to compare him with my midfield partner for Germany, the great Michael Ballack. They were similar in that they were both offensive midfielders and really liked to get forward, which meant that whichever one I played with I didn't have to change my game. Michael was always a great goalscorer and had that special knack of scoring important goals, which is a rare attribute that he shared with Stevie. He could be dangerous from set pieces and was a great header of the ball.

Overall, Michael was a much more economical footballer. He would step back and think about what was going on, carefully picking his runs and thoughtfully selecting the areas that he would cover. Stevie learned to do this over time, but would always have that element of blood and thunder about him, but with such a special engine and the ability to change pace, he could afford that more than Michael. It was more important for Michael to shape his game to work around his limitations and he did that brilliantly.

Stevie Gerrard has been unbelievable for England and it's a real shame that his big moment in terms of winning a tournament has never materialised. He was part of the so-called 'Golden Generation' of English footballers who were meant to dominate the international stage. They didn't and there may be many reasons why not, but it was not for the want of Stevie Gerrard trying.

I hope that England can achieve something on the world stage again. I have to be honest though and say I don't think it's going to happen any time soon. That's not to say England don't have good players, of course they do, but it takes more than good players to get to the business end of a tournament.

One thing I've noticed about England is that there seems to be a need for instant gratification as well as a need to find another all-conquering superstar who is going to bring home the bacon. Such superstars who can pull a mundane team along to a World Cup final probably don't exist. If they do they are freaks of nature. Maradona and Messi are both extraordinary footballers, but even their successes have been achieved as part of very good teams.

Paul Gascoigne epitomises why England can't progress. I don't know the lad, and I know that he has had his problems off the field, so I'm not knocking him. He was immensely talented and a bit of a character too. I'm just saying that if you asked England fans to name recent England greats, Gascoigne's name would most likely get a mention. He's loved in a way that could not happen in Germany.

Had Gascoigne been German he would be persona non grata today. You would never hear mention of his name. I say this because of what happened when England faced West Germany in the 1990 World Cup semi-final in Turin. West Germany had taken the lead early in the second half, only for Gary Lineker to equalise with ten minutes remaining. Perhaps this was to be England's moment. As the game went into extra time Gascoigne, who was already on one yellow card from a previous game, made a lunging tackle on Thomas Berthold. The referee pulled out a yellow card and Gascoigne lost it. He went to pieces as he realised that if England won he would play no part in the World Cup final. The game was still tied, and a job still needed to be done, yet his first thoughts were for himself. His only thought should have been, 'What can I do for my team?'

When the game went to a penalty shoot-out Gascoigne was earmarked to take the third penalty for England. He decided that he wasn't in the right frame of mind to take it so David Platt had to step into the breach and take Gascoigne's penalty. For Gascoigne, in that moment, it was all about *him* as an individual, and the way *he* was feeling. It was nothing to do with his duty to the team. Football is a team game. England seem to live with the continual hope that putting out a group of talented individuals will create a team. It doesn't. Other things have to be in place.

If Gascoigne was German his behaviour would have created a national scandal, and the player would be forgotten for ever. If it were possible to erase his name from the teamsheet then it would be done. He certainly would never be named among the great German players no matter what he had done before, in the way that Gascoigne is for England.

I can say this with confidence because of what happened in the 2002 World Cup. It was exactly the same situation for us. Michael Ballack was on one yellow card and we were facing South Korea in the semi-final. It was a hard-fought game and after seventy-one minutes Ballack received his second yellow card. He knew, just as Gascoigne knew, the massive implications of that card. He would not play in the World Cup final if we were to make it there. His reaction was brilliant. It was nothing less than Germans would expect. His first thoughts were not for himself. He was part of a team and there was still a job to be done. The score was tied and the game was still there to be won. Four minutes later, Michael Ballack popped up and scored the winner. His goal put us in the World Cup final. He was totally selfless. His delight at reaching the final, even though he knew he would not play in it, was every bit as genuine as that felt by the rest of us. Back in the quiet of the dressing room though Michael was heartbroken. That year with Leverkusen he had lost out on the Bundesliga title on the final day of the season, lost the

German Cup final to Schalke and lost the Champions League final to Real Madrid. Now he had to miss the World Cup final. Yes, he shed a tear or two, but only after he had done the business for his team. That's what you call a hero.

Just to reinforce the point, Lothar Matthaus, unlike Paul Gascoigne, has done everything and won everything. He was World Footballer of the Year; won the Ballon d'Or; played in three World Cup finals, winning one; won a European Championship; and that's not to mention the gigantic haul of medals he won at club level. Just for good measure he won 150 German caps over an incredible twenty-year period. In any other country this man would be an all-conquering hero and legend. People in England have received knighthoods who have not achieved even half of the things that Lothar has. Yet, according to press reports, Lothar has put himself forward for more management positions in Germany than anyone else over the past ten years and he has not even got a sniff of an opportunity. Instead he has had a career as a roving manager in the outposts of football from Brazil to Belgrade, Bulgaria through Israel and places in between. The rumours about Lothar's link with *Bild* haven't helped, neither has his celebrity lifestyle. Lothar is something of a Lothario and is already on his fourth marriage and the gossip magazines love to follow his every move. Yet one of the things that Germans cannot forget about Lothar, and will not forgive him for despite everything that he did and achieved, is the 1990 World Cup final that West Germany won. Yes, I said *won*. In the final against Argentina, Lothar was the designated penalty-taker. A stud broke in one of his boots and he was feeling uncomfortable in them, so he passed on his penalty-taking duties to Andreas Brehme with the score locked at 0–0 with five minutes to go and a penalty awarded to the Germans. Brehme scored, we won the World Cup and you would think that would be that. Yet German football has little time for sentiment and as each year goes by it seems that Lothar's few failings, especially the fact that he passed up taking that penalty, are better remembered than his extraordinary achievements. Things like that send out a message to every up-and-coming German footballer. The culture is unforgiving and the culture is not about *you* it is about *us*.

This I think sums up one of the reasons why Germany has been a successful tournament team over the past few decades. We are not looking for an individual saviour, though we produce great individuals, we do everything for the good of the team. It is not an optional extra to be applied when you feel like it. It is something that is absolutely non-negotiable if you want to be in the German national team.

English players have to raise the bar. If an English player breaks into the Premier League today, he is immediately regarded as a success. If he is very good he will be heralded as the new talent that is going to break England's duck. He is immediately given a heavy burden of expectation to carry and, with the riches and media attention that will be thrown at him, he is made to believe he is successful when he is not. Playing in the Premier League indicates only one thing – that you have achieved a high standard as a professional. It means nothing more. It is not the same as success. There is only one measure of success in football and that is winning trophies.

Some English players win competitions with their clubs, but this is when they are in a team of mixed nationalities. It seems that when you put eleven talented Englishmen together you take away an important ingredient. In England they will be regarded as successful simply for pulling on an England shirt; in Germany you have to do much more to get recognition and, more importantly, to feel that you deserve it. Gascoigne, one of England's so-called best players, went through a whole career winning very little – he got an FA Cup winners' medal but was in hospital when it was given out due to a self-inflicted injury that nearly threatened his career, and he picked up some silverware with Rangers.

When your heroes are people who win very little and it's acceptable to shirk your responsibilities to your team when the chips are down because of the way *you* are feeling, don't be surprised if you breed teams that are talented but can't compete at the highest level when it matters.

England seem to be building a 'me' culture that wants to cling to any sort of instant gratification. When we lost 5–1 to England in Munich, the English reaction was to get out the history books and write a new chapter. It was just one game in a long sequence of games towards the World Cup finals and the German reaction was to keep our eye on the big picture and to concentrate on what was important. After that, England made the last eight at the World Cup and we made the final, so perhaps there is a lesson there.

On the tenth anniversary of England's 5–1 win in Munich an English newspaper produced a double-page spread to commemorate it. Commemorate what? England won a World Cup qualifying game, that's all. David Beckham is even quoted in this feature as saying, 'I think about that game almost every day.' He was a great player, a fantastic role model and a lovely lad, but for a former England captain to think almost every day about a qualifier in a year in which England only made it to the last eight reinforces my belief that England and England players have got to start to see a bigger picture if they are ever to do anything that is truly worth writing home about.

The last time England were successful on the world stage it was with a team that showed tremendous dignity, modesty and respect for each other. They had great players who led relatively normal lives, had a culture of humility and self-sacrifice, and an esprit de corps that was once a hallmark of English culture.

That esprit de corps doesn't seem so strong any more, in football or in English society, and that's a problem too because footballers are a product of the society that they grow up in. What I see is a great country that has let its standards slip as the structures that maintained discipline and order in English society are being eroded. What is left is an obsession with instant gratification and a mistaken belief that success is about material possessions. England's on-the-pitch problems, I believe, have as much to do with its off-the-pitch problems and the culture that is emerging on the streets. Though England will continue to produce great players it will not become a force as an international team unless the players can reproduce the sense of self-sacrifice that was the essence of the 'Spirit of '66'. People could argue that the 'me' culture and the obsession with all things 'bling' has come about with the riches of the Premier League and that it is not the players' fault that they earn vast sums of money. I can go along with that. It is not their fault and good luck to them. But most of the Premier League players are now foreigners, and they seem to be able to cope with wealth and still stand up for their country.

I was perhaps Germany's most reluctant soldier, but square bashing did a lot for me as a person at a young age. If England really want to win the World Cup, perhaps now is the time to stop looking for an instant saviour. Perhaps now is the time to bring back national service.

CHAPTER EIGHT

FIRST WE TAKE BOLTON, THEN WE TAKE MILAN

'In which Rafa tells me to go'

I remember staring up at the sky. It was a beautiful, clear Wednesday evening in late May 2005.

'I could think of a lot better places to be on a Wednesday evening than right here right now,' I began to think to myself. This was a funny thing to say really, because as I tilted my head downwards to take in my surroundings, a vast sea of red and white came into view, a wall of noise seeped into my consciousness and I was reminded that I was standing in the centre circle of the Ataturk Stadium in Istanbul, about to start the second half of a Champions League final.

There was just one small fly in the ointment. We were 3–0 down against AC Milan, who were playing as if to justify the commonly held belief that they were the best club side in the world at that time.

It was all a bit confusing in a way, because it was looking

as if I had no future as a Liverpool player. With my contract due to expire at the end of the 2004/05 season, Rafa had spoken to me in January 2005 and we had verbally agreed the basis for a new contract. I was delighted because Liverpool was where I wanted to be. It was to be a one-year deal and if I played a minimum of twenty-five games I was to get a one-year extension. That suited me. I wanted to play and felt I could command a regular place in the team. I trusted Rafa's word and though nothing was said I took it that we had an agreement and that we would do the paperwork towards the end of the season. Paperwork wasn't really my department, I just wanted to play football.

Then we started to go through a really bad patch in the second half of the season. Chelsea came to Anfield and beat us 1–0; as did Manchester United; we lost at Southampton 2–0 and by the same score at Birmingham; we then dropped another Anfield point to Blackburn. A couple of wins in between did little to put a gloss on what was a very poor period by anyone's standards.

Sammy Lee pulled me aside at training in the middle of this bleak period and told me that Rafa wanted a word in his office. I went in and he sat me down and got straight to the point. He said in a quite unemotional tone, 'Didi, I've thought about it. That offer is not an offer any more.'

I didn't know why, but he was ending my Liverpool career and I didn't even argue the toss with him. I just looked a little stunned and said 'OK'. That was it. I walked out of the office.

As Rafa's words began to sink in I realised that in about twelve weeks' time I would no longer be a Liverpool player.

It was a bolt from the blue. It hurt me badly, but I knew that Rafa was a no-nonsense kind of guy and that he had meant what he said. As the weeks went by word began to get around that I was on my way out of Liverpool. Bolton manager Sam Allardyce let it be known that he was interested and he was given permission to speak to me. Sam's proposals sounded promising, so a couple of weeks before the last Premier League game of the season my lawyer went on ahead to the Reebok Stadium to finalise the details of the deal. Meanwhile, I followed on and sat in the car park waiting for him to ring me to tell me that I could go in for a medical. When the phone rang it emerged that Big Sam had thought this through a little more and spotted a potential problem. The problem was not with me or with the deal that he had put on the table, it was simply about the timing of it. The stumbling block that Sam foresaw was due to Liverpool and Bolton being neck and neck on points and vying for fifth place in the league. With clubs receiving more prize money the higher up they finished at the end of the season, a movement upwards of one place could mean several hundred thousand pounds more in Premier League prize money to Bolton. Although we didn't have to play Bolton, Liverpool's result would affect their position. Sam was worried that if I was in the Liverpool team and made a crucial mistake or scored an own goal that it might look a bit suspect, as if we had cooked it up. My lawyer agreed with Sam that we should wait until the end of the season when there could be no question marks placed around the deal. It left me slightly in limbo, but I could see Sam's point and I knew that if I just waited a few weeks then I would be a Bolton Wanderers player. I turned the car around and drove back down the M62 to Liverpool.

Before that final Premier League game at home to Aston Villa, we had the little matter of a second-leg Champions League semi-final at home to Chelsea with the score deadlocked at 0–0.

We had progressed in the Champions League that season and we'd had to show a lot of resilience too. This was becoming a hallmark of our team. We felt that when we were up against it we could always find a way to win. What great preparation that was to prove to be.

We stuttered a little in the group stage as we beat Monaco 2–0 at home, only to lose 1–0 at Stade Louis II. The Greek side Olympiacos gave us a tough time as well, beating us 1–0 at their new Yorgos Karaiskakis stadium. After Deportivo held us 0–0 at Anfield we feared the worst but I think this was a turning point for our campaign as we went over to Spain and beat them at Estadio Riazor 1–0. That was not an easy thing to do and it began to give us a lot of belief in ourselves. After the game Rafa and the Spanish contingent wanted to give us a taste of their culture, and for once Rafa allowed his strict regime to be relaxed a little as he brought in a huge Iberian ham along with the finest Rioja.

Qualification from the group stage came down to the last game against Olympiacos at Anfield. We had lost to them in Greece and with the way the group was poised we could not even afford to draw. It was a case of win or be eliminated, and even winning might not be enough. They were three points ahead of us and had superior goal difference.

It was a complicated scenario with lots of possibilities. If Monaco won their final game they would win the group, leaving us and Olympiacos vying for the second qualifying place. Under that scenario goal difference became irrelevant, because if we beat Olympiacos we would be level on points and under the rules qualification would be decided on a straight head-to-head aggregate score in our two games against the Greeks. Clearly this was all happening in real time and it's a good thing I was on the bench with a calculator.

The Greeks were in a strong position because if it did go to a head to head, their 1–0 in Piraeus was worth more than just the points that they had clocked up in the qualification process. It was a kind of insurance policy whereby they could still lose 2–1 at Anfield and go through.

Things looked bleak for us when Rivaldo slalomed half the length of the pitch and was brought down, earning a free kick. He duly dispatched the free kick, opening the scoring for them after twenty-seven minutes. With the score unchanged at half-time Liverpool launched wave after wave of attack. Substitute Pongolle levelled the score on forty-seven minutes to set the scene for an onslaught on the Olympiacos goal. When Neil Mellor made it 2–1 the place erupted in the way that only Anfield can, but there was an anxiety and nervousness in the crowd's desire for the team to continue the surge forward. Monaco were winning, which meant that a 2–1 win for us would see Olympiacos go through with an away goal. We desperately needed another but time was ticking away. In a situation like this there seems to be only one man made for such moments. With Liverpool four minutes from elimination, he popped up yet again. Steven Gerrard reminds me of the mission statement that used to be stuck up everywhere in the Boeing Aircraft Factory: 'The right part, in the right place, at the right time'. Stevie would get a job at Boeing any time, because yet again he turned up in the right place just at the right time. In the eighty-sixth minute he rifled home the goal that would kill off the Greeks and put us through to the knockout stage of the Champions League. Last gasp it may have been, but they all count.

When we faced Bayer Leverkusen in the 'round of sixteen' in the knockout phase, my mind inevitably went back to our last encounter three years earlier and the 'Collapse of 2002'. Yet again I thought about Houllier substituting me, which was closely followed by the sudden collapse when we had the chance to go through and have every chance of being European Champions.

So here was an opportunity to right that wrong in a way. Inevitably, in reaching the Champions League final in 2002, Leverkusen had attracted the attention of other European clubs. As a result they had lost several of their best players: Ballack had gone to Chelsea, Lucio to Bayern Munich and Neuville to Borussia Moenchengladbach. They were still a good side, not to be trifled with, but they were not the side they had been when they dumped us out of the quarter-finals three years earlier.

After the high drama of the win against Olympiacos we felt that we had every chance to pull off a result. We were comfortably 2–0 ahead in the first leg at Anfield with the game running into stoppage time. That put us in a strong position and with our previous collapse at Leverkusen in the back of our minds we needed to go there with confidence. In the ninety-second minute we got a free kick on the edge of the box. Stevie Gerrard, the natural choice to take the kick, was out injured that night. I stepped up and said I wanted to take it. It was a case of 'do or die'. Here was a chance to put ourselves in pole position for the second leg.

I didn't score that many goals, but I did score a few screamers. This one could have trickled over the line for all I cared, but I hit it sweetly and it flew into the bottom corner. At 3–0 it seemed that we had all but wrapped it up, but Leverkusen refused to be counted out. Jerzy Dudek made an error with a last-gasp effort from Franca to allow them to pull one back. They had an away goal, but we had got our noses in front. There was still a job to be done in Germany, yet in a small way that result and the goal I scored was some consolation for what had happened against Leverkusen in 2002.

When we went to Leverkusen for the away leg, we naturally felt confident. We were beginning to hit our stride as a team and on the night we absolutely outplayed them. I got substituted again in Leverkusen, but this time it was for all the right reasons. I would have had a suspension if I had picked up another yellow card, so Rafa took me off as a precaution, but by that time we were well and truly through to the semi-final. We took the leg 3–1, cruising through 6–2 on aggregate.

Eleven days later, playing in a home game against Everton, I once again ruptured the medial ligament in my knee. What was going on? Had someone somewhere deemed it my destiny not to win the Champions League? Typically with this kind of injury you are out for six weeks, then you have to regain your match fitness and then get yourself back in the team. Taking all of that into account and the way time was marching on, I realised that even if we were to reach the Champions League final I might not even play. However, you have to push these thoughts to the back of your mind and carry on doing what you can do and getting behind the rest of the team. I could only take control of certain things and all that really mattered was Liverpool, not Dietmar Hamann.

When I went to see my specialist in Munich about the injury, he had a look at it and said, 'With this type of injury and your history you have to be very careful. I want to put a plaster cast on it because if you don't look after it you could end up with an unstable knee.'

From my point of view I was going to be out of contract very soon, so my main concern was that I should protect my future. If I ended up with an unstable knee I might not get another contract anywhere, so I told him to put it on.

When I got back to Liverpool, Rafa was not very happy about the plaster cast. I guess he thought that even though the season was nearly over he might still have a use for me at some time.

'Why are you wearing that?' he demanded.

I explained about the possibility of me ending up with an unstable knee, and that given my employment circumstances I was not taking any chances.

He said, 'I want you to have it taken off and get back into training as soon as possible.'

I looked at him. 'The plaster cast is on. If you give me a two-year contract, I'll take it off.'

It was a slightly cheeky negotiation stance from my point of view, but he wasn't having any truck with that suggestion so the cast stayed on until my doctor told me to take it off.

When the cast was off, Rafa made a point of picking up the contract conversation again. 'You know that I'm not happy with you about that cast. As far as the contract goes, I made my decision earlier in the year. Whether you agree with it or not is up to you. But you just have to accept it.'

My last-ditch attempt to stay at Liverpool had been ruthlessly put down by a man who never changed his mind – well, hardly ever.

While I'd been restricted to sitting on the sidelines, the lads had seen off Juventus in the quarter-finals to set up an all-English semi-final against Chelsea. I was not quite ready to play when the first leg came around so I watched a full-blooded and very tight goalless game from the stands at Stamford Bridge. What was clear from this game was that whoever went through to the Champions League final would go through on the very narrowest of margins. The most significant thing from my own point of view was that Xabi Alonso got booked three minutes from time, which meant that he couldn't play in the return leg.

Before the return leg Rafa put me on for the last ten minutes at Middlesbrough playing at centre half. It's the first time I'd ever played in that position and to be fair, by the time I came on the game was practically won, so I just had to move around a bit and make it look like I was a centre half. In reality I hardly touched the ball. But the fact that Rafa put me on made me think that I may again play some part in the Champions League, even though my future appeared to be away from Anfield. I went out that night and had a bottle of red wine, just in case I was called upon for the semi-final.

It was one of those beautiful spring evenings the night that Chelsea came to Anfield for the second leg. Just every so often you sense a feeling in and around a football ground that is different from the normal experience. Even as we arrived at the ground there seemed to be something in the air that night and there was a special feeling about the place. The fans were brimming with excitement and yet full of tension at the same time. It was really highly charged, and definitely the best atmosphere I have ever experienced at Anfield.

Normally when we came out to do a warm-up on the pitch an hour or so before the game there would be about 10,000 people spread around the whole ground, so the stadium usually felt empty. On this night, the stadium felt like it was almost full when we did our warm-up. It was as if people had turned up early wanting the match to start and almost believing that they could will it to start sooner. Anfield always had a great atmosphere but this was something over and above anything that any of us had experienced before. It just oozed into us and you felt that, one way or another, something special was about to happen. An hour before kick-off, Rafa read out the team. I was in. Those ten minutes as a centre half at Middlesbrough were a runout in preparation for this night after all.

Old boys had turned up in force to will us on. Steve McManaman, who had gone to Manchester City, arrived along with Robbie Fowler. They may have been with other teams but something inside them was still Liverpool and they, along with almost a team of other Liverpool old boys, were adding their voices to the mighty throng.

As we prepared to come on to the pitch it seemed that even the rafters of this famous old stadium were shaking, such was the intensity of the crowd. They sang relentlessly and as we emerged from the tunnel we were hit by a wave of noise, which was to continue for the whole night.

It really was a clash of two titans. Chelsea hadn't come to defend and hope to hit us on the break; they went for it right from the kick-off. We countered shoulder to shoulder, man for man. Unexpectedly, after just four minutes Steven Gerrard flicked a delicate ball over the top of the Chelsea defence for the Czech striker Milan Baros to chase. Petr Cech showed no sympathy for his Czech compatriot, darting off his line to absolutely clatter Baros, who poked the ball past him. With Baros flattened, the referee waved play on and Garcia darted in to toe-poke it towards goal. Chelsea defender William Gallas hooked the ball away with what he claimed was a goal-line clearance. But the Liverpool players, the crowd and, more importantly, the Slovakian linesman, said it was a goal.

We were one up early on and the noise from the crowd, that earlier had seemed like it couldn't get any louder, just got louder. Chelsea were not going to lie down because of an early goal and they continued to come at us. Our tackling and closing was frustrating them as we were managing to break up much of their play, yet they were still creating chances. Perhaps the Liverpool players shared the crowd's fervour because certainly in the first half we seemed sharper, more ambitious and higher in tempo. You could almost say we were high on the adrenalin that the build-up and early goal had created.

Chelsea pushed on in the second half with some dangerous counter-attacks. Then came an onslaught. They only needed a goal to go through, the tie was that finely balanced. They were creating chances – first Lampard, then Drogba, and Carragher had to make a telling interception to stop Robben. Chelsea began to lay siege on Jerzy Dudek's goal.

This had been a high-energy game and after my long layoff through injury I was beginning to blow a bit. I'd really only played the ten minutes at Middlesbrough and I started to struggle in a match of this intensity. After seventy-three minutes Rafa could see that I was tiring and brought on Harry Kewell to take my place. I watched from the bench as the minutes ticked by. We were almost there when inexplicably the fourth official indicated that there were to be six minutes of added time. Six minutes. The crowd went berserk. Where had this come from? Rafa, who had been kicking every ball for the whole game, continued to kick every ball and waved his hands around like a trackside tick-tack man.

Chelsea could still go through with just one goal, and deep into added time Eidur Gudjohnsen had the chance. Receiving the ball just yards out, he panicked a bit and whipped the ball across the face of the goal, wide of the far post. It was a chance he definitely should have taken. Those last minutes ticked by very slowly until no more time could be added on; the referee had to blow for full time and Anfield erupted in a way that it hadn't erupted for more than twenty years. Liverpool were back where they belonged – in the final of the Champions League.

It was a truly momentous victory in which we showed our steel and resilience. Even Jose Mourinho could not spoil it with his 'goal that never was' jibes. When the goal was analysed from four camera angles it was still difficult to say with absolute certainty what was what. One thing, though, was clear. The goalkeeper committed to a challenge that should have resulted in a penalty and seen Chelsea go down to ten men. The way we were competing for everything that night it is beyond belief that Chelsea could have held out against us. So really Mourinho should have gracefully accepted defeat because the night could have turned out a lot worse for his team.

As the dust began to settle and we were able to pause for breath it hit home that soon we would be on the banks of the Bosporus. We had thought that we were within minutes of going out of the competition against Olympiacos and yet here we were, about to take on the mighty AC Milan in the final in Istanbul.

For me it seemed like my Liverpool days were over. I was thinking that if they had to end then this would be a fitting way – the final of the Champions League and the possibility of a famous victory. If you have to go then that's a pretty good way to go. But I had no idea if I would be in Rafa's plans for the final. He followed the same routine whether we were in a tricky cup game away to Yeovil or in the biggest final of them all against Milan. As always he announced the team about an hour before kick-off. Simple as that. Nobody knew if they had a place and everybody had to prepare as if they were going to play. So for all I knew I may well have already played my last game for Liverpool. If that was the case then

I would have felt I could have gone out with my head held high having done my bit for the team. But of course, every top player wants to play in and win the Champions League. I was hopeful that I was in Rafa's grand plan.

First, we had to finish off our league campaign, which we did with a 2–1 win against Aston Villa. As it turned out, I didn't commit any horrendous mistakes which could have been construed to have favoured Bolton Wanderers' chances, as Sam Allardyce had worried about. At least I could pick up negotiations with Sam about going to Bolton and begin a new chapter in my life. But for now, with the league programme over, there was only one thing to concentrate on. It was an unusual situation in that we had nine clear days before the final to prepare. That's a long time when you are used to playing every three or four days. With the Premier League finished it felt strange, as if everybody else had gone on holiday and we were left behind. The papers had little else to write about so the build-up was quite intense. The media hype grew stronger as each day passed.

We felt a little like I imagine boxers do in that we had an unusually long time to prepare for a one-off match. We were trying to maintain a high level of intensity in training while being careful not to incur any self-inflicted, reckless injuries. We saw them not as injuries to individuals but as injuries to a team. We had always had a strong sense of 'the team' at Liverpool and I think coming through those very tough Chelsea games and the feeling of achievement of having got to the Champions League final had made that team spirit stronger than ever. We were going to need that to overcome a dazzling Milan line-up.

Normally when you are talking about a great team you highlight a few of their great players. When you looked at the Milan team we were about to face, you just couldn't do that. Dida, Cafu, Stam, Nesta, Maldini, Pirlo, Gattuso, Seedorf, Kaka, Shevchenko, Crespo – how could you pick two or three or even four out of that lot? That was an incredible line-up, a World XI if ever there was one. Yet we felt that collectively we were a match for anyone. We were together and in adversity we always believed that somehow we would find a way, whatever was thrown at us.

This is one of those times when words are not sufficient to even begin to describe what happened next. If the Chelsea tie was immense, then you can share my frustration that words sometimes have their limitations. Words can set out the sequence of events, convey something of the atmosphere, but words have not been invented that will adequately sum up a night that will stay with me until the day I die. And even then there will not be words that help me to describe it.

The Milan game seemed to be an almighty uphill battle even before we were on the pitch, though Rafa was his usual calm self and didn't change anything about the way we prepared for the game. Our training was the same and our travel arrangements and routine were the same. Then about an hour before we were to set off for Istanbul's Ataturk Stadium, he broke his pattern and did something unusual. He asked us all to come downstairs into a hotel meeting room. It was set out like a small cinema. We settled down and Rafa said, 'We are going to watch a little film.' He had compiled highlights and goals from Liverpool's famous history as European champions. For many players in the foreign contingent the history of Liverpool was known about, but it was history, it didn't resonate in the same way as it did for the home-grown boys. So we started with the 1977 European Cup final 3–1 win against Borussia Moenchengladbach. That was Kevin Keegan's final game for the club. Would this be my last game for the club? I still didn't know if I would be picked to play. Then we saw the 1978 final and a 1–0 win over Club Brugge, with Kenny Dalglish, the man who brought me to England, giving notice that he had no intention of playing in the shadow of Kevin Keegan. The 1981 final showed Liverpool overcoming the 'big guns' of Real Madrid. The conclusion was the 1984 final against Roma. That was a win on penalties against an Italian team, in which the keeper, Grobbelaar, played a big part. A premonition perhaps?

Maybe what Rafa was trying to do was to infuse the history of Liverpool into the team, and all of us, not just the foreign contingent, were reminded that we were a part of an amazing dynasty. You might have expected Rafa to give a long speech or tactical talk at this point, but what he did hit just the right note. He simply said, 'Tonight, we can write history. Let's go.' With the benefit of hindsight that was an incredible line. So off we went, buoyed up by witnessing the glory that was in our footballing DNA and with a simple, clear message in our minds that whatever may happen, 'tonight, we can write history'.

One hundred thousand Liverpool fans made the journey to Istanbul that night and only 20,000 had tickets. The city was awash with red and white and there was no doubt that we were involved in a massive occasion. Inside the changing room Rafa followed his usual routine and waited until an hour and fifteen minutes before kick-off to announce the team. If I had to play my last game for Liverpool I wanted this match of all matches to be my last.

Everybody wanted to be in the team, more now than ever. I'm not one to blow my own trumpet, but I did know that I had had a very good game in the second leg against Chelsea, even though I wasn't fully match fit after my injury. I'd been substituted in the semi-final, quite rightly because I was definitely tiring. Yet I fully expected to be in the team for the final. Rafa began his announcement, 'Dudek, Finnan, Traore, Carragher, Hyypia, Kewell, Gerrard, Alonso . . .'

My stomach churned. I didn't hear any more after that. I knew at that moment that I was on the bench. It hit me like a hammer blow. I tried not to show my disappointment. I have Gerard Houllier to thank for the way I dealt with it. Gerard used to say, 'If you are not picked to play in the team, you have two minutes to get over your disappointment. Then you get your head up and prepare as if you are going to play. Otherwise it is not fair on your team and if you are asked to come on and you are not in the right frame of mind you let your team down.'

I can't say that I didn't have a problem with not being picked for that match. I did. I was devastated, but I allowed my devastation to last only two minutes just as Gerard had said in the past. Then I prepared as if I was going to play. I was on the bench, so it was not inconceivable that I might come on at some stage.

Down on the bench we could barely believe what we were seeing. Within just a minute of the kick-off a free kick from Pirlo was met by Maldini who volleyed sweetly, high past

Dudek. Disaster; we were 1–0 down against a very powerful and skilful team in less than sixty seconds. The only saving grace it seemed was that we had eighty-nine minutes to get one back.

An early goal can happen. Sometimes it can be a bit of a blip. But this was no blip. Milan were absolutely buzzing. Crespo and Kaka were flying. They were playing the sort of stuff that has you in awe. At times in that first half I would say that was as near to a perfect performance as you can get and for periods the dominance they showed was almost embarrassing.

In the thirty-ninth minute Shevchenko broke away down the right flank in a sweeping attack, and crossed for Crespo to turn home from close range – 0–2. Five minutes later, Milan added a third when the Brazilian Kaka, the most influential player in the first forty-five minutes, unlocked our defence with a brilliant pass that released Crespo for a clever chip over the onrushing Dudek.

We sat on the bench stunned. There was a quietness on the bench the like of which I had not experienced before. Partly we were in awe of what Milan were doing and partly we were puzzled thinking. 'What's gone wrong?' When the third goal went in I thought, 'Well thank fuck I'm not playing.'

We all trudged into the dressing room. There was chatter among the players, but nobody was chatting about anything other than what they thought was happening out there. Rafa walked in looking quite calm. I think he had already made his mind up about what he was going to do the moment that third goal went in.

He looked over at me. 'Kaiser, you get ready, you are coming on.' Then he turned to Djimi Traore and said. 'Djimi, you are coming off, go and get showered.' Rafa reacted in exactly the same way as he did when he made substitutions on any other day. 'Go and get showered.'

I whipped off my tracksuit and began to head outside to do a warm-up during the half-time break. As I was heading out I saw Djimi walking semi-naked towards the showers. I winked at him and he nodded as he pushed back the shower-room door and disappeared. His night was over and mine was about to begin.

And then there I was, standing in the centre circle of the Ataturk Stadium thinking, 'I could think of a lot better places to be on a Wednesday evening than right here right now.' The Liverpool crowd had somehow set aside their shock and despair and had lifted themselves. They were alive to the sound of 'You'll Never Walk Alone', almost hoping against hope that somehow, some way, they could lift their team.

What can you do in a situation like that? You have to think about what is realistically achievable at that point. My thoughts were that we had to try to get one back and if we could do that it would be a good start. If we carried on as before it would end up as a humiliation. The fans would never forgive a humiliation. I did think though that they would forgive us if we at least made a fight of it, and if we could get a goal back then that would be something. This was not the way I imagined my last game in a red shirt to be.

I'd gone through my warm-up and the players began to emerge for the second half. I couldn't believe my eyes when I looked across to the tunnel and saw Djimi Traore walking on to the pitch getting ready to play. I had heard Rafa telling him to get showered, I walked by him and saw him as he was walking into the shower room semi-naked. Had he gone mad? What was he doing? I thought maybe the occasion had got to him or something.

I stopped Carra as he was walking past. 'Hey Carra, you had better have a word with Djimi. This is going to be embarrassing, we are going to start the second half with twelve men. We will look like we don't know what we are doing.' I think all of our heads were in a bit of a whirl and maybe I wasn't thinking straight.

'No, don't worry, Kaiser,' said Carra, 'Finn's had to go off injured and Rafa got Djimi out of the showers.'

With my confusion sorted out I just wanted to get started and see if we could do something for our supporters – give them something to cheer and avoid a humiliating defeat even if we could not avoid defeat altogether. Rafa's battlecry that 'tonight, we can write history' seemed a million miles away. Was it a million miles away? Maybe not. Maybe it was lying dormant somewhere deep in our collective subconscious. Maybe it was just waiting for something to spark the idea into life.

I dug in to try to tighten up our midfield, which gave Stevie Gerrard more of an opportunity to push forward. If anyone had a chance to make something happen it was Stevie, who was clearly hurt by what had happened in the first half. Nine minutes into the second half Stevie threw us a lifeline. Bombing forward he met Riise's cross on the move and headed into the far right corner of the Milan net. An inspirational captain had written the first paragraph of history.

Stevie ran back to the centre circle with such a look of

determination on his face. His arms were flailing like a rampant butterfly as he urged every one of us to find something extra within ourselves. We surged forward from the kick-off and within two minutes Vladimir Smicer, who was on for Harry Kewell, hit a speculative shot. Dida got a hand to it but fumbled it into the net. This was incredible. We were now within one goal of pulling back what had seemed like an impossible deficit only eleven minutes ago.

Now I thought, 'Anything is possible from here.' Milan were rocked and there was an opportunity for us. On fifty-nine minutes Stevie was put through again and was sure to equalise only for Gattuso to pull him down for a stonewall penalty. In the space of six minutes we had gone from facing one of the greatest humiliations in Champions League history to the possibility of producing the greatest comeback in Champions League history. It was all down to Xabi Alonso. If you had scripted this to produce maximum drama, then you would write in a spot kick like this one. Alonso hit the penalty kick well only for Dida to parry it. Even in the heat of the moment Xabi had the presence of mind to follow up and he pushed the rebound home.

We were incredulous. How had this happened? What had we done? Can we go further and win it? Milan looked shattered, but even though this was a devastating blow for them you couldn't count out a team of that quality. Although we felt we maybe had the momentum with us to go and win it, they were not going to lie down.

The emotion of the comeback and the sheer physical effort, I think, had drained us more than Milan. With the score 3–3 at full time we went into extra time. With about five minutes to go I felt a little crack in my foot. I wasn't in a tackle or anything like that, my foot just landed on the hard surface of the Ataturk pitch and something cracked. I found out later that it was a hairline fracture of a metatarsal in my right foot. It hurt for sure, but I was in no doubt that on this night of all nights, in this game of all games, I was carrying on.

Inevitably in this remarkable game there was to be yet more drama. With one minute to go, Andriy Shevchenko had the most incredible chance to win the game for Milan. A couple of yards out Dudek saved from him low, Shevchenko hit the rebound high and somehow, I don't know how, Dudek recovered and denied him a second time. Even when you watch the replays of that double save it seems unfeasible, as if there was some kind of electromagnetic force field protecting our goal.

Dudek had kept us in it.

Extra time for us was really about hanging in there and trying to get to a penalty shoot-out. When the final whistle came we were out on our feet. We had given everything and, win or lose, what we had achieved was phenomenal. Yet I felt that we had every chance at this stage, because Milan must have been thinking that they should have been celebrating victory by this time. It must have been playing on their minds and doubts inevitably would have been creeping in.

The period between the final whistle and the start of the shoot-out must have lasted about six minutes. I remember that I adopted the same attitude that I always did in the dressing room before games. I kept quiet and tried to focus on what needed to be done. As far as I was concerned nothing was settled and we still had a serious job to do. I walked around to try to clear my head and as far as I am aware I spoke to only one person.

Rafa came over and asked me a question. 'Do you want to take a penalty?'

I had a broken bone in my foot, although of course Rafa was unaware of this, but I said nothing about it and had absolutely no hesitation in replying 'Yes'. I carried on with my solitary thoughts. A few minutes later Rafa came back across to me. 'You're taking the first penalty,' he said. That was either an inspired decision or a peculiar one. I don't know which. I wasn't really a penalty-taker. I'd only taken a couple in the whole of my senior career and I missed one of those in the League Cup final against Birmingham.

But I was ready to stand up and be counted for my team. I figured that psychologically Milan must be feeling a bit fragile now, and if I could get us off to a good start it could be instrumental in furthering the doubts that were inevitably beginning to grow in their minds.

Serghinho took Milan's first penalty and missed. I didn't stop to analyse whether that was a good thing or a bad thing for me as I prepared to take our first penalty. You can over-complicate things and get yourself in a muddle. During my quiet time walking around the pitch in preparation for this moment I had decided upon a simple strategy, 'Score'. I knew if I could score this first one it would be like hammering a nail in their coffin. If I missed it would give them a glimmer of hope.

I looked from the ball to the goal. 'It's only twelve yards,' I thought. That's about the length of an average-sized living room. But it seemed like a long, long way away. Dida, the six feet, five inch goalkeeper, looked more imposing than ever. I looked at him and it appeared that there was hardly any space between his head and the crossbar. Had he grown? I couldn't let all of these thoughts mess up my simple strategy, so I thought to myself, 'If he doesn't move early I'm going to my left.'

The moment came. He didn't move early, I hit the ball to the left and in it went. It was a massive relief. Milan must by now have gone from disappointment to near devastation.

Just before we left the hotel all of us, including Jerzy Dudek, had watched the antics of the Liverpool keeper Bruce Grobbelaar in the 1984 European Cup final against Juventus. Grobbelaar had feigned having spaghetti legs as he faced the Italian penalty-takers. Jerzy reckoned that movement might just put off the Milan penalty-takers, especially given the 'backs against the wall' position that they now found them-selves in.

Something had an effect on Pirlo, who took the second Milan penalty, because he missed and piled even more pres-sure on them. This was followed by Djibril Cisse's successful spot kick, which turned the screw a bit more. Milan had gone from a seemingly unassailable position to the brink of disaster. That must have been messing with their heads.

Tomasson scored for Milan, and then John Arne Riise's miss gave them a slight glimmer of hope. Kaka scored. Smicer replied. It fell to Andriy Shevchenko to keep them in it. He could have settled the game on several occasions during normal time, and had the chance of a lifetime followed by a second chance of a lifetime in that final minute of extra time. Dudek had so far denied him his moment of glory.

Jerzy was moving to and fro in the centre of the goal. Shevchenko moved purposefully forward, tried to remain level-headed and placed the ball. Surely Dudek could not deny him again. He did. Dudek saved. He saw us all charging towards him. He had been so wrapped up in the game he had not realised the implications of that save, so he looked like a frightened rabbit, unable to comprehend why we were charging at him like the Light Brigade. It was the save of saves. The save that clinched our great comeback, in what must have been one of the greatest matches of all time. Liverpool were European champions for the fifth time, and the trophy would be coming home for good.

Every emotion and feeling that you can describe or imagine, we had gone through it that night: anticipation, hope, shock, confusion, awe, determination, anger, despair, relief, joy, elation, togetherness, incredulity. These are just a few of the things that we were feeling on a night that, had it been scripted for a made-for-television film, the critics would have slaughtered it and laughed it off as being 'too far-fetched'. Far-fetched it may have been. A near impossibility at one stage had become a reality. At half-time English bookmakers were offering odds of 395–1 against a Liverpool victory. That's how unlikely and incredible a story this was.

That night, one moment summed up the genuine link between the Liverpool players and the Liverpool fans. The fans were not simply people who helped to pay our wages, they were part of the Liverpool family. Once the players had embraced Jerzy for his magnificent performance, they charged over to embrace the fans with an intensity of a mother whose son has just returned from war having been presumed dead.

It was not a case of us, the players, celebrating for our fans. We were celebrating together. We were as one. It was our victory, all of us together.

Everything after that is hazy in my memory. We were out there celebrating on the pitch for maybe an hour. The game finished at 12.30 a.m. local time, so it must have been about 1.30 a.m. when we eventually made it back into the dressing room.

The match itself was incredible but taking into account all that had happened, when I walked into the dressing room it was one of the most extraordinary things I have ever seen. After all of the hurly-burly and the high drama that had gone on out on the pitch, when we got back to the dressing room everything went strangely quiet. There was a hushed atmosphere. People were talking quietly among themselves. Some were sitting silently, staring into the middle distance trying to take in what had just happened.

I sat on the changing-room bench, reflecting for a moment, when I saw the Liverpool chairman David Moores come in. He had a big smile on his face and tears were running down his cheeks. He had been chairman for fourteen years at that stage, and no way in his wildest dreams could he have imagined a night like this. Nobody could have imagined a night like this.

I watched as he made his way across the room, shaking hands and hugging people as he went along. When he got within earshot I leaned over to him and said, 'Chairman, I need to see you in my office for a moment.' I gave a surreptitious nod towards the showers.

After all that had happened everybody was in a state of shock and confusion, most especially the chairman, and he just didn't get what I was on about. 'Your office?' he said. 'What do you mean?' He took it seriously, as if somehow I might have established an outpost of Hamann plc deep in the underbelly of the Ataturk Stadium and having won the Champions League I now wanted to get on and transact some important business.

I gently guided him towards the shower room. 'I need to see you *in my office*,' I said, winking and making the sort of face that said, 'Just do as you are asked, it's urgent.' He stood with me in the shower room looking confused, but he tolerated my odd behaviour. We had become pals because we had something in common. We were the only two people in the club who smoked.

Having bundled him in I said, 'Chairman, I need a cigarette; quick, let me have one of yours.'

He looked at me as if I had asked him to let Milan take the cup home.

'But Kaiser,' he said, with the whispered sense of urgency of a naughty schoolboy, as if he would be in trouble if anyone heard, 'I can't do that. What if Rafa comes in?'

Unbelievable. I was now speaking with a whispered sense of urgency, but more because I was gasping for a cigarette than through fear of being found out.

'Chairman,' I said, 'you own this fucking club. Remember? If he comes in you just say "Kaiser's having a cigarette" and we take it from there. OK?'

He reluctantly agreed and pulled out his pack of cigarettes. It was then that I noticed the state that he was in. His hands were shaking so badly he took ages just getting the packet open. Eventually, I stepped into a shower cubicle and the chairman lit both of our cigarettes. We both took a long, long drag and then we just looked at each other for what seemed like an age, him with tears running down his cheeks, shaking so badly that the ash from his cigarette was falling to the floor at will. We stood looking at each other in total disbelief.

For a long time he looked at me and I looked at him. Nothing was said. The look between us said everything. Not a word was spoken. Because there were no words that could describe what it was that we were feeling.

Him and me; me and him; us, and all the people in the dressing room; all the people making their way through the ancient streets of Istanbul; people going berserk in pubs, clubs and living rooms across the world; an unknown comedian who had decided that his life had to change; we were all experiencing a similar feeling. A feeling that defies description. A feeling that is priceless.

We were Liverpool. We were the champions.

This night, we had written history.

CHAPTER NINE

RAFA'S REPRIEVE

'In which Rafa tells me to stay'

I was totally wrecked. Two days after that incredible night in Istanbul, Rafa asked to see me. I don't think I'd slept for about thirty-six hours, and when I walked into Rafa's office I must have had the look of a Sunday pub-team player after the end-of-season party.

I can't tell you much about what happened after David Moores and I finished that illicit cigarette in 'my office' at Istanbul's Ataturk Stadium. It is a blur. I know that we went back to our Istanbul hotel in the early hours of the morning and celebrated with friends and family. I know that we partied on the plane home, and I remember that I did not sleep very much at all. There are a few times in your life when you can be excused for saying that events are a blur, and I guess that this is one of those times. Everything was a bit of a blur. I make no apologies.

When I heard that Rafa wanted to see me I came to my senses a little. I thought, 'Well he either wants to say goodbye, or I have got one last chance to change his mind about me leaving.' I had nothing to lose. I headed for his office determined that I would try to change his mind.

I bowled up with something of a casual air. 'What's the sketch?' I said. I thought I'd act pretty relaxed and informal. Then I thought that I'd better stop being nonchalant and make my position absolutely clear. 'I don't want to go,' I said quite firmly. We were like two lovers on the verge of separation, getting ready to divide up the CD collection, perhaps each hoping that the other would propose a reconciliation. Unashamedly I had blinked first. It was true, I didn't want to go.

After all we had been through together on the Wednesday night, Rafa showed no emotion. He was totally businesslike. 'I'll give you the same offer that I took off the table earlier in the season,' he said.

Well at least this was an improvement on no deal at all. I thought back to the offer that he had coldly withdrawn a few months back. This meant a one-year deal, with a clause saying that if I played twenty-five games or more I would automatically get another one-year extension.

Maybe it was the lack of emotion in Rafa's approach, I don't know, but I felt that I had to let him know how I felt. I was always one to put the team first, but I had to get this off my chest. I said, 'I expected to play on Wednesday. You withdrew the contract and I still played my part against Chelsea. I expected to play in the final.' He remained impassive but I was getting into my stride. 'What would have happened if I had said "put someone else on" at half-time on Wednesday?' I asked. I even felt like saying, 'What if I had said "put yourself on"?' But I restrained myself. I knew in my own mind that never in a million years would I have said that, but I just wanted him to be aware that despite the fact that he 'pulled' the contract I continued to give my all for the team. I just wanted to sow the seed of the idea that we wouldn't be sitting here looking at the Champions League trophy if I hadn't done that.

This riled him a bit and for the first time there was a spark of emotion 'No. No. No. The team comes first. Never think about yourself. The team comes first and then after that comes nothing,' he said.

That shook me up a bit because nobody had to tell me about being a team player. Everything I had ever done at Liverpool had been about the team first and foremost. I said, 'Come on, after what happened on Wednesday we have to change the clause from twenty-five games to something lower so that I have a good chance of getting the one-year extension.'

Rafa reasoned that because there was no rule that the champions had automatic entry into the following year's Champions League, we might be allowed to play from the first qualifying round, so there would be a lot of games that I could possibly play in.

I still felt, particularly after all that had happened, that I deserved better treatment than I was getting from Rafa. I felt that I had a right to fight my corner so I said, 'Come on, let's knock it down to eighteen or twenty games and I'll sign.'

Rafa had reverted to his default unemotional stance, and mulled over my suggestion for a moment. Eventually he gave way, but only a little. 'We make a compromise,' he said. 'The follow-on clause kicks in at twenty-two games. That's it.'

I think if I had left it there and said 'I'll think about it' or even declined the offer, Rafa would have come under a lot of pressure from the fans and the media. I could have taken a risk and hoped that people power would turn the screw a bit more. But with this offer I saw the chance to play for another year and then get a year's extension that would have seen me finish my career at Anfield, and that is what I wanted to do more than anything. I loved the club. I didn't want to go and play somewhere else, even though I could have left on a massive high as a Champions League winner. Anfield was where I wanted to stay as long as I could keep on playing regularly.

So we shook on it. Rafa's new deal requiring me to play twenty-two games in order to get an automatic one-year extension was sealed. Three days earlier I was on my way out, most probably bound for Bolton Wanderers. Now, incredibly, I had been drawn back into the Liverpool fold. Result.

I staggered out of Rafa's office with deep black rings under my eyes and eyelids that were beginning to feel like lead weights, but also with a smile as wide as the Mersey. I went straight home to bed and for a moment I lay looking at the ceiling. I was happy, exhausted and still slightly delirious. As I drifted into a half-sleep I wondered if all of this could possibly have happened. 'Please tell me this is not a dream,' I said to myself, and then I was away with the fairies.

The season after our European triumph was memorable for our FA Cup run. I say memorable, it's all a bit of a blur too really. I don't remember that much about our run to the final, largely because I was a spectator for most of it.

I know that I watched a traditional 'ding-dong' of an FA Cup encounter at Luton, when at one stage it looked like we might be heading for a shock exit as we were 3–1 down. A second-half revival saw us come away with a 5–3 win in a match that had everything you would want in a cup tie. I had more spectating to do at Portsmouth, in which we battled for a 2–1 win only to be awarded the booby prize of a tie against Manchester United. The only upside was that the game was at Anfield and on this occasion I was in the team. These are never easy games but Peter Crouch put us ahead after nineteen minutes and we managed to hold on to the lead to earn a quarter-final tie away to Birmingham. I was back in the stands for this one and watched almost in disbelief as we slammed seven goals past Birmingham at St Andrews to sail through to the semi-finals along with Middlesbrough, West Ham and Chelsea. Out of the three of them there was one team that we definitely wanted to avoid, but the magic of the cup pitted us against them. It was to be Liverpool versus Chelsea at Old Trafford. This time I spectated from the substitutes' bench and watched us come through a vibrant and hard-fought encounter with a 2–1 victory.

We had to face West Ham in the final and though we were never overconfident, we felt that we were the better team in the run-up to the game. We felt confident that we could win this one. We had beaten Milan a year earlier in that momentous game in Istanbul and I and many others believed that we now had an even better team than we had then. I started on the bench so I had a pretty good view of what was going on.

The way I see it is that West Ham could have and should

have lifted the FA Cup that afternoon. They were well prepared, extremely professional, everything that they were supposed to do they did and they made very few mistakes. We did make a few mistakes, and an own goal by Carra put the Hammers 1–0 up before Dean Ashton made it two. We managed to pull the game back to 2–2 but as West Ham's Konchesky looked to cross the ball, it fluked over Pepe Reina and went into our net. With a 3–2 lead they must have been putting the claret and blue ribbons on the cup as the game moved into stoppage time. Rafa had brought me on in the seventy-first minute for Peter Crouch; a midfielder for a forward in a situation where we had nineteen minutes to get a goal struck some people as an odd thing to do.

We looked dead and buried, but something about the spirit that had developed after our legendary win in Istanbul would not allow us to believe it. Then came the mistake that cost West Ham the cup. It was a simple but monumental mistake born out of naivety really.

As a player went down injured, the West Ham goalkeeper, Shaka Hislop, tapped the ball into touch just twenty yards from his goal, when he had every opportunity to punt it into touch way over the halfway line and into our half. I immediately ran over to retrieve the ball to take the throw-in. Carra came running over to me. 'Kaiser, Kaiser, don't throw it out for a goal kick.'

Obviously the correct thing to do in this situation is to return the ball to the opposition to resume play. Carra was worried that because it was close to their goal that I would throw it out for a goal kick, thus giving them a chance to slow play down. I'd already thought this through and I said,

'Don't worry about it, that's why I came over here to take the throw.' With the injured player now recovered, I took the throw-in so that it dropped in front of a West Ham fullback but I made sure that it didn't have sufficient weight on it for him to shepherd it out for a goal kick. I gave him a respectful one and a half seconds to contemplate the ball and then immediately closed him down, putting him under sufficient pressure that he had to make a long clearance into our half.

Immediately the ball was returned back into the West Ham eighteen-yard box and cleared only as far as the man you would want to receive the ball with the final whistle about to blow any second. Steven Gerrard has done some inspirational things in his time, but his powerful drive from thirty yards into the left-hand corner of the West Ham net has got to go down in his greatest hits. He was Mr Boeing once again. He was 'The right part in the right place at the right time'.

Shortly afterwards the final whistle blew and with the West Ham players dealing with the devastation of being so near yet so far, we had the momentum. In extra time both sides began to feel the effects of what had been a pulsating game played under a baking-hot sun. Lots of players were going down with cramp and nobody could really get into a rhythm. I inadvertently handed West Ham the chance to wrap it up in extra time. I gave away a bad free kick over on the right; it was a little rash. The cross that came in flipped off someone's head. From where I was standing I felt sure it was going in until Pepe Reina produced an incredible fingertip save to knock the ball on to the post. He got me out of a hole there and it was another occasion when I realised that small things can make a big difference in turning a game. If their keeper had not made the error of not kicking the ball into row Z in the final minutes of normal time, and had our goalkeeper not got the finest of fingertips to the ball in extra time, the result could have been different. But these fine margins went in our favour, and when it came to a penalty shoot-out I definitely felt confident that we could come through.

Just as in Istanbul, Rafa decided who the penalty-takers were going to be. As captain, Stevie Gerrard had a decision to make and came over to me. 'What do you think we should do, Kaiser?'

I was in no doubt. 'I'd like us to start; let's see if we can take the advantage.'

My thoughts were that West Ham would be just like Milan at this stage, they would be feeling pretty devastated having virtually had one hand on the cup. If we could put them behind on penalties it would just keep them under pressure.

I wanted to take the first one, so when Rafa told me that I would I was happy with that. This time there was no broken bone in my foot, but that didn't make it any easier. I wanted to give us the psychological advantage.

Shaka Hislop was trying to tease me by not standing centrally, positioning himself to one side of his goal. He was only a couple of inches off-centre, but as far as I was concerned I wasn't put off, I just saw it as an opportunity. I thought I'd just keep it straightforward and go into the corner where he was leaving me the space. I suppose that's not rocket science, but you have to keep it simple otherwise you start to confuse yourself and that's how you end up missing. I hit it cleanly as I had planned and it was in. I think that was a hammer blow to the Hammers, because of the four penalties they took after mine, they missed three. Their resolve had been broken. Their hearts too, probably.

As I sat in the dressing room and pondered on how games can turn on such small incidents, I began to think about the West Ham players and how they must be feeling. I'd never felt sorry for Milan when we beat them in Istanbul. They had the players to beat anyone, the experience and the lead, so I had little sympathy for them. I did feel sorry for West Ham. They had done everything properly and they had played like a team that played in finals all the time. On the balance of play they definitely deserved to win the game. In the end experience, resilience and the confidence that comes from winning things tipped the balance in our favour.

That was an unusual moment for me having been brought up with a winning mentality at Bayern Munich and Liverpool. Suddenly, for a moment, I was thinking about the team that came second. It wasn't the only unusual thing that occurred that day. I was unaware of it at the time, as I straightened my tie and gathered a few belongings, but this was to be the final time that I would leave a football ground as a Liverpool player.

We had pulled off yet another triumph in winning the FA Cup against the odds, when all looked lost. It was becoming a trademark of the club. We came back to Liverpool in the usual high spirits and there was a celebratory meal laid on for us.

You never get tired of celebrating a victory. When we won

the Champions League in 2005 that was some celebration, yet so were all of the others, and German players know how to shift a few beers too. Yet for me the FA Cup win in 2006 had a different feel. We were celebrating for sure, but it all felt a bit subdued to me. I'd played enough games during the season to kick in my automatic one-year contract extension, so there was no reason for me to feel anxious or subdued. The players, wives and girlfriends were all there as usual, but to me something felt different and I just couldn't put my finger on it. I tried to get on and party as normal, but something just wouldn't let me break loose. Then a strange feeling came over me. The hubbub of the celebration seemed to fade into the distance. I seemed to float away from the action and it was as if I was looking down on events from somewhere up on the ceiling. I sat back, and although nothing had been said, I found myself thinking, 'I've just played my last game for Liverpool.' This was an illogical thought because I had the security of my contract extension. Why was I thinking like this? I just felt a kind of sadness inside and although I went through the motions of the celebrations, a feeling inside me was trying to tell me something.

Back at the training ground Benitez asked to see me. He had put the clause in the contract and we had agreed that if I played twenty-two games then I got an automatic one-year extension. That season I had played in thirty-two games and made twenty-odd starts, so I knew that I could activate the clause and stay another year. He sat me down. He wasn't suggesting that I should not activate the clause, he just wanted to let me know his plans. 'Next season I want to bring in a winger and move Stevie into the middle. That means that you won't play so many games,' he said. Obviously, as a player you want to play as many games as you possibly can. The thing I knew about Rafa was that he didn't fanny about. If he told you something it was dead straight. He didn't do the mind games, he just played everything with a straight bat. I always respected him for that.

So I started to realise what he was saying. I had every right to stay, but to stay and play maybe fifteen games, that wasn't me. I didn't want to become a bit-part player and have people saying, 'Oh Didi, he was great for us once but he's past it now.' That just wasn't for me. The scenario Rafa was painting would have seen my Liverpool career simply peter out with a whimper and I couldn't bear to think that things would end like that.

I explained my thinking to Rafa. It was a hard decision for me to make and I didn't want to say these words but I felt that I had to. I said, 'I think I would be better going some-where else.' As is his way he showed no emotion, even though I think he knew that this was a big call for me; he just wished me well. But that was Rafa, businesslike until the end.

Those strange feelings I had at the FA Cup-final celebration and the realisation that I had played my last game for Liverpool seemed as if they were a kind of premonition. Even though I had no way of knowing that this was to be the end of the line for me at Liverpool, something in my gut had told me that it was.

I was sad and disappointed, but it's like Gerard Houllier used to say, 'You can be disappointed for two minutes then you must prepare.' There was a future to be had, somewhere. There was a new chapter to be started. I had my two minutes of disappointment. I allowed myself the luxury of a few moments of reflection on the wonderful years I had enjoyed at Anfield, and then I began to feel a tinge of excitement.

It was lovely to look back on that amazing time at Liverpool, but I reminded myself of something that I believe in – my interest is in the future, I intend to spend the rest of my life there.

CHAPTER TEN

ONE-DAY WANDERER

'In which I become the world's most expensive free transfer'

The phone rang. It was a withheld number. 'Don't tell me, I've won another free double-glazed window in return for spending twenty-five grand on uPVC,' I thought. Yet something told me that I should answer this call, so I picked up the phone and hesitated, half-expecting to hear the monotonous patter of a double-glazing salesman.

It surprised me. It was an interesting call from an unexpected person. The caller spoke with a soft Scottish brogue that sounded familiar. 'Didi. It's David Moyes here. I'll cut to the chase, I'd like you to come to Everton.'

What? This was a difficult one. I've got a lot of respect for David Moyes, I think that he is a really good manager. I'd always enjoyed our encounters with Everton too, they were great games and great occasions. The Everton fans had always been fine with me as well, so I had no problems there. Despite the massive rivalry in the city, I had never had one single moment of trouble with any Everton fan.

Obviously, word that I was leaving Liverpool had started circulating on the grapevine. I would have very much liked to have played for David Moyes. The problem was it was Everton. As all of this was swirling around in my mind, I think my gut instincts just did the talking for me. 'Moysie,' I said, 'I'd love to play for you, but I want to be able to go back to Liverpool in the future. In five or ten years' time I want to go back and be treated as one of the family. If I play for Everton, I could go back, but I don't think the feeling would be the same. I would jeopardise my relationship with the club that I love and that's not something I want to do.'

I really didn't want to jeopardise that relationship for the sake of a year, maybe two. Things would never have felt the same had I put on an Everton shirt. David Moyes understood. It was flattering to have a manager of his calibre wanting me to go to Goodison. Had it been anywhere else I would have quickly been into detailed discussions with him.

I had to say no to Everton, but I knew that Big Sam Allardyce had kept his ear to the ground. He had missed out on signing me twelve months earlier because he wanted to ensure that nobody could have any doubts about his conduct or mine in the event that Bolton finished above Liverpool in the table.

As things panned out, Rafa's reprieve meant that he had lost out on my signature, but he quite understood my position. Who wouldn't have stayed at Liverpool given the chance and the circumstances?

Sam had let it be known that there was a place for me at Bolton Wanderers on exactly the same terms as he had offered on the day that I had sat in the car park at the Reebok Stadium waiting to go for the medical that never happened. That was a big gesture from a big man. I wanted to stay in the north-west as well, so Bolton seemed like a good option. The club I really fancied was Manchester City. I'd played a preseason friendly there when I first arrived at Liverpool and I had liked it ever since then. They had moved to a new stadium and I always thought of it as a big club. Of all the clubs within striking distance of my Wirral base, Manchester City was the one I would have preferred to go to. Steve McManaman and Robbie Fowler had gone there too, so there was a Liverpool connection about the place.

City knew of my availability and never called, so quite naturally I assumed that there was no interest there. I arranged to go to Bolton to speak to Big Sam and to have a medical. Sam was true to his word and he laid out on the table a contract with exactly the same terms as he had set out just over twelve months earlier. I completed the medical with no problems, signed the contract and we shook on it and agreed that we would see each other at preseason training.

I told Sam that I was heading straight off to Munich to be with my family, but as I was leaving he called in one of his backroom team. 'Just show Didi round the area. He's off to the airport, so you go in your car and he'll go in his, just give him a quick whizz around so he can get a feel for the area.'

When we left Sam's office it was quite a pleasant day weather-wise. I followed the car in front of me and was given a running commentary over the phone as we drove through the suburban districts of Bolton. 'And over here on the left,' says the phone commentary, 'is where Jussi Jaaskelainen lives.'

It was nice enough. Then as we were driving along the sky turned a deathly black. I've never seen sky like that before. It was like something out of a biblical epic. Great drops of rain began to fall until, even with the wipers on super-fast, I could barely see where I was going. It made the whole place seem bleak. They call this the land of dark satanic mills and I could now see why. Something was gnawing away at me inside. My gut was telling me that something about this wasn't right. Surely this downpour, that felt as if Armageddon had arrived, wasn't some kind of a sign? I don't think so, but something about it spooked me a little, to the point that I was wondering if I had done the right thing after all. Doubts suddenly began creeping into my mind.

I was living on the Wirral at the time, which meant that I could hit Manchester in an hour and it was probably another half an hour to Bolton. My marriage was going through a difficult patch, and the bleakness of the whole place was not filling me with enthusiasm. But I had signed the contract and as far as I was concerned that was that.

By now I'd seen enough. I thanked my escort for showing me around and headed for Manchester Airport to catch the late-afternoon flight to Munich, where my family were waiting.

I didn't have much time to ruminate on the decision that I had made to sign for Bolton, because within five minutes of setting off for the airport my phone rang. I saw on the display that it was Robbie Fowler and thought he must be ringing me to wish me a good summer – nice. I answered. 'Eh Didi. I'll get straight to the point. I've been talking to Derek Fazackerley at City. Do you fancy going to City? Faz says they would be interested if you were.'

I couldn't believe it. There I was having doubts about Bolton and now there's a chance to go to Manchester City. Perfect timing. Well it would have been perfect timing if I hadn't already signed Sam Allardyce's contract. Then I thought, hold on, this could be manna from heaven. This could be just one of those things that is meant to be. Go along with it and let's see what happens.

'Look Robbie,' I said, 'I'd love to come to City. Tell Derek that I'll come, but he must get Pearcey to ring me up within the next hour because I am very close to signing for Bolton.' It was a little white lie, but I was putting the ball in their court. If they wanted me, someone would have to work out how we could make it happen.

Half an hour later Stuart Pearce, who I'd played with at Newcastle, called up. 'Pearcey, I want to come. I'll come for exactly what I've been offered at Bolton,' I said, and I told him the details. He agreed and I told him I was about to get on a plane and that I would ask my lawyer to get in touch to sort out the details. I had not mentioned the fact that I had signed for Bolton already. Why spoil a good conversation?

I just had time to ring Andy, my lawyer, who couldn't believe what he was hearing. 'What? You've signed for Bolton and agreed to go to Manchester City. Are you mad? How the hell am I supposed to deal with that?'

I didn't have time to debate it with him, my plane was getting ready to leave. 'Andy, I have no idea how to do it. That's what I pay you for.'

As I boarded the Munich plane, Andy began a delicate process of shuttle diplomacy.

About a week later we were all sitting in Big Sam's office

in Bolton. I came clean with Sam. I told him, 'Sam, my marriage is on the rocks, my wife's planning to go back to Germany with the kids. When you are not in a good frame of mind you can make poor decisions. I think that's what I did. I just can't see myself coming here.' I told him that City would match the terms he had offered me and that I didn't want to go there for more money. It was just that I felt it would be better for me and it might give me a chance to keep my personal life on an even keel.

You might have expected Sam to hit the roof at this point, but he was quite understanding considering the circumstances. He weighed up the situation, came to terms with it in his head and said, 'Well, we will want money for you.' Andy helped the two clubs sort it out. City agreed to pay Bolton Wanderers £400,000 for a man who had never kicked a ball for them, had never even been to training and hadn't even made it as far as the payroll. I was like the invisible man. It's been dubbed the most expensive free transfer ever.

If City had only rung an hour earlier they could have had me for nothing, and I would even have taken less money, so keen was I to go to City. Think about that; that hour's delay in making contact with me ended up costing them £400,000. That's £400,000 an hour. That's more than some lawyers earn. In the event I'd ended up in a shade of blue that would be more acceptable on my return to Anfield than the blue of Everton and David Moyes. So that was satisfying too. Although I feel that I would have done a good job for Bolton, the prospect of playing for Manchester City filled me with an excitement that I hadn't felt at Bolton. It was not a 'head' thing, it was a 'heart' thing, but I'd noticed that in the past when I had listened to my instincts, things had usually turned out for the better.

I'd played with Stuart Pearce at Newcastle United for a season and I liked him. He was, as you would expect, straight as a die and no-nonsense. His playing reputation had left him with the nickname 'Psycho' and he was certainly never half-hearted in a tackle. At Newcastle he trained exactly as he played. It was comical sometimes when a ball came over and the cry went out 'Pearcey's', you would see people cringe, duck, get out of the way – anything to avoid being another one of Psycho's victims.

In the dressing room though, he was much more considered and quite low-key. He would speak up if something important had to be said but otherwise he blended in with the group. He had a bit of a passion for music, which he didn't try to impose on other people. His music taste tended to reflect more of his on-field Psycho-type personality than his off-field gentlemanly manner. He was into bands like The Clash – very appropriate for somebody that went into tackles the way he did. It was edgy punk rock in the main that caught his interest. Can you imagine going to a punk concert with Pearcey? I never did, but I wouldn't have liked to have been standing in front of him when the pogoing started, you would have ended up in hospital. Maybe that's why punk died out. Pearcey probably hospitalised the lot of them in one mammoth pogo session.

I liked the set-up at City right from the start. They were a big club and as soon as I got there it felt good. They had a few crazy characters that made up for the absence of Carra in the dressing room. Ben Thatcher was chief among the mirth-makers at the City of Manchester Stadium, as we called it back then. Richard Dunne became a good mate, he was solid as a rock on the pitch and a big, soft teddy bear off it. Then there was the bizarre world of Stephen Ireland, who could make me laugh whether he intended to or not. So right from the start I felt at home at City.

After years of success at Bayern Munich and then Liverpool, this was a new challenge and a new experience for me. I was enjoying the new environment. As a footballer you have to get used to settling in with new faces all of the time, so that was OK as well. But we got off to a slow start. We lost 3–0 at Stamford Bridge on the first day of the season and had patchy form from there, which meant that for much of the season we were trying to steer away from the relegation zone.

Then there were the moments when you realise that you are not thought of in the way that you were once thought of, perhaps. I'd been injured in a preseason game in China, but I was ready for our fourth game of the season, which was against Reading. We had chalked up four points from three games, so a win here would see us heading in the right direction. I was one of the substitutes. Reading went 1–0 up after only twenty-three minutes, which wasn't a disaster but it didn't help our cause. Then they had a man sent off and were struggling to break out of their own half. I thought that this was the ideal situation for me to be introduced into the game. My holding play, I felt, was just what was required to allow other players to move forward and overwhelm Reading with pressure. This was a game that was winnable, I thought.

I watched slightly bemused as one substitute after another was called from the bench and sent on, while I remained sitting there in a game that I felt was crying out for someone who did what I knew I did well. I didn't know if it was because Pearcey didn't see me as a mainstream part of the team or whether he just didn't see the tactical possibility that I felt was pretty obvious. When the final whistle went, ten-man Reading had managed to hold out for what I thought was an unlikely 1–0.

Winning that game could have given us seven points from four games and maybe would have given us a lift. Instead we ended up with four from four and after that we were scrapping for a point here and a point there. I found myself in and out of the team too, which was a new experience that I was having to get used to.

Off the pitch that season, Ben Thatcher led the merriment in and around the City changing room. Ben was a bright lad who had dropped out of Canterbury University in order to turn professional with Millwall. He was just the kind of uncompromising defender that Stuart Pearce would approve of. In fact, he was maybe a little too uncompromising, even for Pearcey. In the preseason we went out to China for a couple of games. In a match against Shanghai Shenhua, Ben led with an elbow in a challenge against Shanghai's Yang Chungang, putting the poor lad in hospital with a career-threatening collapsed lung, and this was in a friendly.

Three weeks later, in just the second game of the season, the Thatcher elbow made a return appearance, this time right in front of the TV cameras in a home match against Portsmouth. In a challenge for a loose ball with Portsmouth's Pedro Mendes, the elbow flashed again and knocked Mendes into the advertising hoardings, rendering him unconscious. He suffered a seizure on the journey to hospital and was in a bad way.

Ben got hit with a six-week suspension by the club plus the maximum fine of two weeks' wages. City probably saw this as a Cantona-like moment and tried to mitigate the damage prior to the FA taking a view. The FA gave Ben a further eight-week ban plus a fifteen-week ban suspended for two years. Now he had to think more carefully about what he was doing. He did tell me though that he had no memory of the elbow incident. It was almost as if he had blacked it out of his mind. Sometimes things do happen in a flash and you react to situations almost unconsciously. Whether Ben could recall what had happened or not, he was not going to be playing for quite some time.

Despite the ban, Ben continued to be an entertainer around the club and had a special relationship with City's legendary kit man Les Chapman. Les probably knows more about the game than any kit man anywhere. He should do, he played an amazing 747 football league games for eight different clubs and had a season in the USA with San Jose Earthquakes. This was before going into management with Stockport County and Preston North End. After coaching City's youth team he didn't want to stop being involved so he became the kit man.

He and Ben Thatcher enjoyed a bit of banter and one day in the canteen Ben started a new Manchester City tradition. Les was going on about the lily-livered players of today and made the mistake of saying, 'You lot, you don't know you're born. You can't take your drink. Me, I've got a constitution of an ox I have.'

Ben saw this as an opportunity for some fun. He looked at Les and said, 'Reckon you can drink anything, do you?'

Les was a proud northerner and he wasn't going to give

an inch to this soft southern upstart. Les didn't flinch. 'Anything,' he said, grabbing a cup from the canteen drinks station. 'Whatever you put in that cup I can drink it and hold it down,' said Les. With that he banged the cup on the table and stared at Ben as if to say 'go on, I dare you'.

Ben grabbed the cup and went behind the cafeteria counter. He started by pouring in a small amount of coffee to which he added some Tabasco, sugar, mustard, salt, pepper, lemonade and then some tomato ketchup for good measure. He then stirred the concoction and put it in front of Les to really test his northern resolve.

Les looked at it slightly apprehensively and said 'hold on, hold on', which was greeted by a barrage of catcalls from the lads that had gathered around to see what was happening. But Les wasn't backing out, he saw an opportunity. 'I'll drink that,' said Les, 'but you lot are going to have to put your hands in your pockets for charity.'

Everybody wanted to see this, so someone got a bowl from the crockery pile and began passing it around. Ben counted the money. 'There you go Les,' he said. 'You've got no excuse now, there's two hundred quid there for your favourite charity.'

Les looked determined as he said in his broad Lancashire accent, 'Reet, here goes.' He picked up the cup, took a deep breath and took his first gulp. His eyes went round in circles but he got it down. Two more gulps and it was gone. His stomach retched for just a moment then he gained control and slammed the cup on the table. 'There. Told you,' he said. The lads erupted and Les took his money to his favourite charity.

If ever we needed a laugh, Ben would go around the changing rooms with a hat and we would head up to the canteen with Les. Each time the concoction grew more and more bizarre. Although Les struggled from time to time, he never once failed the task, and he raised thousands of pounds for charity in the process. It was true, he did have the constitution of an ox.

By the time November came, we were scheduled to go to Anfield. Although I realised that I wouldn't always be in the team, this was one occasion when I especially wanted to be selected. I wanted to play in front of those fans at Liverpool who had become so special to me, an amorphous mass of people who I regarded more as friends than as a crowd. In the end I got on to the Anfield pitch for the warm-up but that's all. I got a nice reception, but spent the rest of the game on the bench. Someone once said, 'All you get at Anfield is a cup of tea.' It was one of those days for us, because we didn't get any points or any goals. We lost 1–0 to a Steven Gerrard goal. It wasn't the return to Anfield that I had wanted in any sense. Losing was bad enough, but being a spectator sitting on the substitutes' bench was not the way I wanted it. I would have to wait a little longer for a playing return to Anfield.

As the season progressed there were rumours that the club would be taken over by the former prime minister of Thailand, Thaksin Shinawatra. This eventually came about. We continued to toil away, and it really did feel like we were toiling at times, coming in at fourteenth place. Goals had been a big problem for us and our top scorer ended up being Joey Barton, a midfield player with six goals, so that shows how powder puff we had been in front of goal. We just didn't have that cutting edge, scoring a measly twenty-nine Premier League goals all season, joint worst with Watford who finished bottom. Our only saving grace was that we were able to keep a clean sheet when it mattered, so we nicked a few 1–0 wins and 0–0 draws, otherwise we would surely have been relegated.

It wasn't quite dismal, but it wasn't great and the incoming owners were beginning to put it about in the press that they were in the market for a high-profile manager with an international reputation. The writing looked like it was on the wall for Pearcey, but one of the great truisms is that the league table doesn't lie. Over that season fourteenth was a fair reflection of what we had and hadn't done. We were struggling for players, to be fair. Pearcey had been tied to quite a frugal transfer budget and with us finishing fourteenth he was not going to be given a chance to bring any more players in.

We went off for the close season, and really as a player you don't know any more about what is going on than the average fan. The only information we have is the stuff we pick up from the newspapers and maybe a bit of gossip, but no more than that.

Football is an unsentimental business. When the papers announced that Pearcey had been replaced by Sven-Goran Eriksson I was just glad that the uncertainty had ended and something had been settled so that I knew when I was due in for preseason training and who I was going to be working for. That's no disrespect to Pearcey, it's just better if things are settled.

I was intrigued about the idea of working under Sven. I'd only met him once before. A German delegation was invited to 10 Downing Street before the 2006 World Cup. In the evening we were given a reception in London and Sven was there in his capacity as England manager. We had a chat for about ten minutes, mostly about the weather I think. I came away with a good impression of him. He was a nice fella as people had said he was.

It's funny when you look back on meetings that you have with people that seem to be of no significance, then years later you find that the person is to play an influential part in your life.

That's the way it was with Sven. Our paths were destined to cross again more than once after that brief encounter in London. The next time would be in Manchester, basking under Sven's 'Blue Moon'.

CHAPTER ELEVEN

SVEN'S BLUE MOON

'Sverige's svelte Sven spots a new career option'

From the outside looking in it must have seemed like a soap opera at Manchester City: a former Thai prime minister for an owner, a charismatic charmer for a manager and a group of fans starved of success living in the shadow of Manchester United.

Yet for the players all of this goes on in the background and you just try to get on with your work. Sven kept Derek Fazackerley, who had been assistant to Stuart Pearce, so there was some continuity about the training, but brought with him the men who went everywhere with him – fellow Swedes, Hans Backe and Tord Grip. A nice touch was that Sven was first there every morning waiting for the players to arrive and as always was calm and charming. His serenity is legendary and it was helping to create a lovely atmosphere about the whole place.

Unlike Pearce, who desperately needed reinforcements,

191

Sven was given the luxury of spending big as the new owners wanted to make an impression. He had about £40 million at his disposal and I've no doubt that Tord Grip played a part in deciding who to bring in. The Italian Bianchi was the most expensive signing at £8.8 million, coming in from Reggina. Two Brazilians came in the form of Elano and Geovanni. Corluka and Petrov were bargain buys and then Gelson Fernandes, Garrido, Bojinov, Caicedo and Benjani followed.

Having brought in new faces, the thing that Sven did with ease was to bring the whole club together. From the cleaning lady to the receptionist to the temporary loan signing, Sven had a knack of making everyone feel welcome, wanted and cared for. One of the loan signings Sven brought into the academy was a young man from Inter Milan, by the name of Mancini, the son of an up-and-coming manager. It was a name that was destined to ring around the corridors of Manchester City in the years to come.

After a year in the doldrums suddenly, with this atmosphere and this squad, it just felt great. I had the feeling that I was back in the big time again before we had even kicked a ball in anger. There was a real buzz about the club and I think the fans were feeling it too. As the season started we got off to an absolute flier. Two of the new boys, Bianchi and Geovanni, weighed in with goals at West Ham as we kicked off the season in style with a 2–0 away win. Another clean sheet in a 1–0 win at home to Derby County, followed by the same score against our rivals Manchester United, saw us go top of the league. Nine points from nine and not a goal conceded. City fans were in 'Blue Heaven'.

We had a few setbacks during the season, but were holding

our own and managing to stay in the top four or five. On a cold January afternoon we made the trip across the Pennines to play Sheffield United, and bizarrely got beaten by a balloon. Exuberant fans had been releasing balloons into the air and the occasional one came down on to the pitch. One balloon landed in our penalty area and as our keeper attempted to make a clearance the ball rebounded off the balloon and went through his legs and into the goal. It's not often you get nutmegged by a balloon, but over the years 'shooting yourself in the foot' had become a part of Manchester City folklore and this was one more crazy episode to add to the list. To be fair though, Sheffield United were sharper on the day and deserved their win. Having been dumped out of the FA Cup by a balloon, by February the lack of strength in depth began to tell and our challenge for a top-four spot started to slip away.

On 10 February 2008 there was a particularly poignant moment and I was honoured that I was able to play a part in it. Four days earlier it had been the fiftieth anniversary of the Munich Air Disaster, a devastating tragedy in which twenty-three people were killed on the way back from a European Cup tie in Belgrade. Eight of the dead were Manchester United players and another three were backroom staff. The fixture list, either by accident or design, had matched us against United at Old Trafford on this momentous day. As a kid in Munich, I was only vaguely aware that something bad had happened somewhere in the dim and distant past, but as I established myself in England I became more aware of what had happened. It must have been devastating for the club and for the city.

The rivalry between the City and United fans is immense, and in the run-up to the game the papers were full of stories about a supposed plot among City fans to disrupt the minute's silence that was planned before the match. The very idea was causing outrage among the United fans. As we came out on to the pitch in front of 75,970 passionate red and blue fans, United in their replica 1950s kits and everyone wearing black armbands, there was a degree of tension. I hoped desperately that the City fans would show proper respect, but nobody knew what was going to happen. The referee blew his whistle to mark the start of the silence and now we would find out the truth. Both sets of fans were spot on in their behaviour. The silence was impeccably observed and was a fitting tribute to all those who had gone before us. Sad as it was, it was a memorable day and both sets of fans showed that there are things that are bigger than football rivalry.

We had a team full of experienced players who could handle a big occasion and on that day we played particularly well as a team. United's Ronaldo had been rampant during the season. He was always going to be difficult to tame, but in this match if ever he beat one man there always seemed to be another one backing up. Of course, United always have eleven match winners in their team, but if you could keep Ronaldo quiet then you at least had a chance of doing something. By half-time we were 2–0 up and it was a lead that we held on to. Michael Carrick scored for United in the ninetieth minute but it was too late for them to come back and we ended up deserved winners.

On the anniversary of the Munich Air Disaster the man from Munich was given the man of the match award. I was delighted to receive it and in a way it was quite a poetic turn of events. Shortly afterwards, Sven extended my contract for another year, even though there were murmurs that Sven might not be around.

The United game was a highlight but the truth was that we were slipping away from the leading pack in the Premier League. Things weren't helped when in February Sven felt that he had to make an announcement to the team. There had been some speculation in the press that Shinawatra was in trouble, and that his reign may be short-lived. There was also speculation about the stability of Sven's position. He came into the dressing room and acknowledged the rumours and said, 'Whatever happens you must finish the season well, even if I am not here to see it. We must all play for our futures.'

A lot of us were unhappy about the shabby way in which Sven was being treated, especially as there was no reason to change anything. He had done as good a job as anyone. He had put City on an even keel after years of lurching from one manager to another. Sven looked like he was the man who could create stability and put a smile on everybody's face at the same time.

Sven's announcement was understood, but he was so well liked by the players that I think some were quite dismayed by the thought that he would be replaced. I think that may have lost us 1 per cent of an edge, just at the time when we were falling away a bit after our whirlwind start.

There was another guy at City who brought a smile to my face. I just had to look at him and at times I just couldn't help myself, I would have to laugh. He didn't even have to say anything, you just knew by looking at this lad that he was a character. Stephen Ireland is a really lovely lad and a good guy to have around. He can be a tremendous player. The funny thing about him is that he is a bit eccentric. He has his own particular taste, which I think can best be described as Hollywood meets Bollywood with a twist of County Cork. Stephen changed his cars more often than he changed his underwear. He never had just normal cars. One day he came in with a blinged-up black Range Rover with shocking-pink spindle wheel trims, matching pink grille and pink side-vent trimmings. You can imagine the stick that he got at a testosterone-charged training ground when he pulled up in that. He looked like an advert for the Irish branch of Sheilas' Wheels. Yet the stick that he got from the other players didn't bother him, in fact I think he got a kick out of it.

Ben Thatcher had a couple of young kids and I guess he spent a lot of time with them looking at furry animals. He also had good powers of observation and he noticed something that reminded him of a creature that his kids might have considered cute and that we found hilarious. According to Ben, Stephen had the look of an otter. With his shaven head, wide eyes, receding chin and darting movements, you can actually see the resemblance. Once Thatch said that then everyone was on to it and Stephen began to be known as 'Otter'. All he needed was a fish in his mouth. Sometimes I used to think that Stephen needed someone to talk to so that he could think things through, so I tried to be there if I could. Some of his views about things I think were quite weird and sometimes bizarre. Maybe that's why he needed a sounding board from time to time because I think sometimes he found it difficult to differentiate between what was weird and bizarre and what was reasonably normal.

There was one occasion that he got himself into an almighty tangled mess. He had played only six times for the Republic of Ireland, but he had done well and scored four goals. You would have thought that here was a lad on the brink of a successful and rewarding international career.

In September 2007 my former teammate Steve Staunton was managing the Republic of Ireland and had selected Stephen for the squad to face the Czech Republic over in Prague. While they were out there Stephen's girlfriend rang up to say that his maternal grandmother had died. Steve Staunton immediately agreed that Stephen could return to Ireland and even went as far as chartering a private jet to take him there.

Somehow the media must have got a sniff that something wasn't right and discovered that his maternal grandmother had miraculously risen from the dead. Either that or she had never died in the first place. Stephen then said that actually it was his paternal grandmother that had died and that he had made a mistake. The media were in no mood to let this go away quietly. They tracked down his paternal grandmother and discovered another resurrection from the dead. Most of us would have said 'Fair cop' at this point but not Otter. He then said that one of his grandfathers had got divorced and it was his second wife that had died. The media were all over this like a pack of foxhounds, only their prey in this case wasn't a fox, it was an 'Otter'. They had him in their sights and this time they snared him good and proper. His grandad's second wife provided a third comeback from the grave. I don't know if by this stage he had run out of grandmothers to kill off, or if he just felt it was time to hold up his hands, but Stephen finally admitted that he had wanted to return from Prague to be with his girlfriend in Cork. A psychologist once calculated that if you tell a lie you have to tell seventeen lies to cover it up; then for each of those seventeen lies you have to tell seventeen other lies to paper over those cracks. An accumulator equation of that magnitude would give a computer a headache. Imagine what it would do to the tiny brain of an Otter. No wonder Stephen went into a grandmother-induced meltdown.

That was the way Otter was; bizarre and unpredictable, but eminently likeable. About a week after he came clean to the press we were in the changing room at Fulham getting ready for the game. There was an hour or so before kick-off and I was in my usual routine of sitting quietly by myself, trying to get into the right frame of mind for the game. Otter came over and sat with me. 'I've been thinking, Kaiser,' he said. 'Do you think I should retire from international football?' This was a funny one, the very idea of a twenty-two-year old who had played six games for his country thinking about retirement. I asked him why he was thinking that way and he came clean. 'You see I don't like staying away from home,' he said, as if his parents had banished him to a brutal boarding school. So was that the real issue that he was hiding behind his death-defying grannies?

I tried to help him to think it through. I said, 'If you've got doubts make a clear decision. But think about this. Do you want to play for your country and are you good enough to qualify for a major tournament? That's what playing for your country is all about. Right now I think you have a team –with the likes of Richard Dunne, Robbie Keane and yourself – that has got a chance of going to a tournament. That's where you really test yourself as a footballer. You have to think about that, but it's your call.'

His little otter-like eyes remained wide open while I spoke, and then he twitched his otter-like nose, sniffed a couple of times and said, 'Thanks. I'll think about that.'

He obviously thought about it and subsequently retired from international football at the tender age of twenty-two. I have to say I didn't agree with that, but it had to be his decision and I left him to make it in his own way. It is a bit strange though to become a professional footballer and not realise that a lot of the time you are going to be away from home. Taking the Otter's approach one wonders where would it all end? 'Oh boss, I only want to play home games, and the missus doesn't like it if I play night matches because she has a facial on Tuesday nights and wants me to be there for her.'

Seriously though, there is a little sense in what Stephen says in terms of the way international qualifiers work. There is far more travelling than is necessary. If you are in a EURO or World Cup qualifying group these days you can end up going all over the place. It could be managed better and the travelling cut down. Since the break-up of the USSR there are now fifteen new national teams and Yugoslavia has broken up as well as Czechoslovakia. With the greatest of respect, a lot of these countries are not top notch on the world stage and added to the likes of San Marino, Andorra, the Faroe Islands and Luxembourg, there is room to introduce a qualifying tier for these nations. Look at what happens now. Players have to travel unnecessarily to places like this for little reason. If you analyse which teams emerge from the group stages to the finals, there is usually only one surprise team out of sixteen or so, and it's never one of the minnows.

So why not do something to limit the amount of miles that players travel and, more importantly, the amount of time that they spend travelling? It would be good for the players and the fans. I think that the football authorities should look at this, not least because we all know that footballers tend to adopt each other's trends and the last thing we want is a spate of grannies meeting an early demise.

Otter was given a note from his missus that allowed him to join us for City's penultimate game of the season as long as he promised to be home in time for *X Factor*. It was a game that was of great interest to me. It was at Anfield, and was an opportunity to do what I wasn't able to do the previous season and play once again on the Anfield pitch in front of the Liverpool fans. Just as Stuart Pearce had done the year before, Sven put me on the bench, which was a big disappointment. After an hour Sven turned to me and said, 'Kaiser, get warmed up, you are going on.' As I warmed up I wondered how the Anfield crowd would react to me. I knew they wouldn't boo me, but I wondered if I had just become a distant memory, one of the hundreds of footballers who had come and gone over the decades. Perhaps a ripple of applause would be in order.

I stood on the touchline waiting for permission to come on and felt a few butterflies in my stomach. There was a tinge of excitement about running out on to this particular piece of grass one more time. The referee signalled to me and I jogged on. A small wave of applause began. It built as cheers began to ring out until a wave of appreciation swept the ground. The whole of Anfield rose to their feet and applauded the substitute. It was a tear-jerking moment and images of the night that we wrote history in Istanbul came flashing into my mind. I was in a game and didn't have time for tears, but it was such a significant moment for me. It confirmed to me that wherever I may be and whatever I may do, I would always be a part of the Liverpool family. That meant so much to me. I was so pleased that I had been able to play again at Anfield and even though we lost 1–0 to a goal by Torres, I was made up with the reception they gave me. I had proved to be an exception to the rule that the only thing you ever get at Anfield is a cup of tea. I got a standing ovation that I will never forget. Thank you Liverpool fans.

Our final game of the season was at Middlesbrough and we lost 8–1. The press speculation was that this was the City players' official protest against the seemingly inevitable dismissal of Sven. That's not true at all. It is true that we abhorred the idea of Sven's dismissal, but I put the hammering that we took down to just being one of those things. It was the last game of the season with nothing to play for, so some players may not have been quite on their mettle; we were a little deflated about Sven's position so that may have taken away another 1 per cent; we had a man sent off after just fifteen minutes, which gave us an uphill task; and Middlesbrough just had a game in a million when everything they hit just flew into the net.

Nobody went out to deliberately lose that game. We wouldn't have been doing Sven or ourselves any favours in doing so. It was just a very bad day at the office.

As the season came to a close, Thaksin Shinawatra had arranged for us to play a couple of friendlies in Thailand. It's not really the kind of thing that you want to do at the end of a long season, but the owner wanted his pound of flesh. By this time Sven knew that the writing was on the wall for him, but he remained the consummate professional. My kids were over in Germany and I was anxious to get over there and see them. I went to Sven and asked him, 'Sven, do you think I could slip away to Germany rather than go on this trip?'

He mulled it over almost like Poirot the detective and finally concluded, 'Well. I'm going. I will leave it up to you, but I advise you to go.'

Sven is a man whose advice I will always listen to and so I set off with the rest of the squad for Thailand. It was a relaxed trip, with two showpiece games. One was against a Thai League All Star XI and the other against a Hong Kong Invitational XI, and we dutifully lost both games 3–1.

We all knew that these were almost certainly Sven's last days as the City manager, yet during our time in Thailand he never changed his demeanour at all. One morning I was on a sun lounger by the pool when I saw Sven walking towards me carrying a silver tray with a bottle of champagne and two glasses on it. It was still only ten o'clock in the morning. On seeing him with the champagne, my first thought was that Shinawatra had summoned Sven to a meeting and that he had had his contract extended.

Sven came over and put the champagne on the table next to me, then placed one glass in front of me and the other by his lounger. I looked up and said, 'Boss, what are we celebrating?' I expected him to make the triumphant announcement that he was staying at City.

He turned to me and smiled that gentle smile of his and took on the air of a Buddhist philosopher as he said, 'Life, Kaiser.' Then, after pausing for dramatic effect, 'We are celebrating . . . life.'

That seemed like a pretty good reason to me for a glass of bubbly, and with that he began to pour the champagne.

With a glass of champagne in hand, he stood and looked out towards the horizon. He took a deep breath, then he spoke in that higgledy-piggledy Swedish accent. 'You know Kaiser, I like this place. I think I will manage for another five years and come back here and live with two women. Yes. I think I need two beautiful women.' For a man with a globe-trotting career, and a reputation with the ladies, that sounded like a natural career progression.

He was a man who loved life and it was impossible not to like him and to love being in his company, and it was Sven who got me thinking about my own career options. He switched from being Buddhist philosopher to fortune-teller as he gave me his vision of the future. 'One day Kaiser, I can see that you will be a brilliant manager. I have had only two people with me during my career that never moved but were always in the right place. One was Dunga, who manages Brazil. The other is you.' That was some compliment from a man who has seen a lot in his career. I still had another year to play at City, but that got me thinking about what my future might hold.

As soon as we got back from the Thailand trip Shinawatra wielded his axe and on 2 June 2008 Sven became another statistic in the Manchester City managerial merry-go-round. Two days later Mark Hughes was appointed as the new City manager after a successful spell at Blackburn where he consistently got them to punch above their weight.

As I approached my third season at City, incredibly I was about to play under a third manager, but I always treated these situations as an opportunity to see another style and another way of doing things. The City soap opera continued, with Shinawatra selling out to the Abu Dhabi United Group for Investment and Development. The deal was signed on transfer deadline day at the world's most expensive hotel, the £2 billion Emirates Palace in Abu Dhabi. This was a sure sign that Manchester City were going to have to get used to big numbers. Shinawatra had taken City to a new level in terms of what he was able to spend. Now the Abu Dhabi money made that look like peanuts. It seemed like it would be too late to spend any of it though, with the takeover being finalised on transfer deadline day. Incredibly, it was announced that at a transfer fee of £32.5 million, Robinho had signed for City from Real Madrid in the face of a bid from Chelsea. These people meant business.

During that season Mark Hughes spent £125 million on eleven new players. Stuart Pearce must have been turning in his dugout. In his final season he was able to spend £3.5 million. City had entered the stratosphere. The question was, could it be translated into results on the pitch?

Under Mark Hughes it was a frustrating year for me. I was in and out of the team, and although I felt I was playing well and should have played more often, City now had other options to choose from. In Nigel de Jong they had acquired a player who very soon established himself as one of the best midfielders in the Premier League, he was a great buy. As for Robinho, nobody was quite sure whether he was Mark Hughes's choice or just a trophy purchase imposed by the new owners.

Robinho was a nice lad. Even though he didn't always look that happy on the pitch for Manchester City, he always seemed happy in training. His English wasn't great and he hung out with the other South American lads like Elano and Zabaleta. I don't think the Premier League suited him to be honest, it was a bit too physical for him. Then again, I don't think he had been doing himself justice for a while. He had his moments at Real Madrid, but his scoring record of one goal every four games wasn't that great for a player who was meant to be up there in the world pecking order. He scored a few for City but struggled to make a real impact. I think he's got great ability, but if you can't deliver consistently and be a leader in your national team you aren't in that world top twenty, which is where people often suggest that he belongs. He's a nice lad, with a great talent, but I think his transfer fee doubled when City came forward for him.

Despite my own frustrations about being in and out of the team there was a memorable moment when one day I got a phone call from a film producer. 'Kaiser,' he said, 'we are making a film called *Fifteen Minutes That Shook the World*. Carra and Stevie are going to be in it, but we really need you.' That was a funny one. I'd maybe exaggerated on the odd occasion when I'd been fouled, but I certainly never thought of myself as an actor. It sounded like it could be a bit of a laugh and it was for the charitable foundation that Carra had set up to help kids in need, so I felt a strong sense of wanting to help out.

The film was a comedy tribute to our momentous and historic achievement in Istanbul. Our part of the film centred around what Rafa Benitez might have said in the changing rooms at half-time with us trailing 0–3 against Milan. Rafa's lookalike, actor and comedian Neil Fitzmaurice, was incredible, and me, Stevie and Carra all had small speaking parts.

The scene depicted Rafa giving a comedy rendition of 'My Way', with a Spanish guitarist playing in the background. Meanwhile, a Liverpool player lay on the treatment table cuddling a blow-up doll. Djimi Traore was carried into the dressing room inside a cardboard box with his legs sticking out, at which point Steven Gerrard said, 'Djimi, that's the best you've been in the box all night.' Every time Rafa asked Carra for his opinion he just uttered, 'I'm chokka.'

In response to Rafa's plea for greater effort, my moment came. I was standing up and had to turn to the lads on the changing-room benches and say, 'It's true. We must regroup, if we go down, we go down fightin'.'

I had one line. That's all. But I must have been there for eight hours as we tried to get it just right. One person or another would burst into hysterical laughter every five minutes and there was lots of stopping and starting, trying to get camera angles and lighting right. One of the crew had a pack of cigarillos and I must have smoked the whole pack during all the hanging around that I had to do.

Rafa's lament included 'What is Hamann, what has he

got? He drinks, he smokes, he uses pot. But he will shine, he'll close our ranks. He'll be like Rommel in his tanks.' I let this go, but I should point out that I have never taken pot. It helped the rhyme to work, so I just treated it as a laugh.

I didn't bother checking the script or the storyboard of the film, I just thought that I would turn up and do as I was told, which is what I did. I was unaware that the scenes with a character called McTaggert, who was a whisky-drinking parody of Sir Alex Ferguson, and the Liverpool-hating character dubbed 'Rat Boy' would be quite so cutting. You can see the funny side of the Ferguson and Neville scenes, but had I still been at Liverpool and had I known what the script was I'm not so sure that I would have done it. I can see how it could have been seen as derogatory, but in a way it's a backhanded compliment that these two were picked out for a bit of banter.

The film proved to be a small interlude in a mixed campaign at City. We had mixed fortunes in the league, but had progressed well in the UEFA Cup, having qualified because we came sixth in the Fair Play League the season before. All of the five teams above us had already qualified for Europe so we sneaked in almost through the back door.

Interludes were becoming important to me and I'd always kept in touch with one of my great mates, Michael Owen. At Liverpool we lived close to each other and we would play golf at least twice a week. Michael loves his sports, is highly competitive and is pretty good at everything from darts to table tennis to snooker. And I thought I was a bit of an all-rounder with my cricket. When he went to play for Real Madrid we kept in touch but obviously our golfing had stopped.

There's nothing false about Michael, he's exactly as he appears to be – presentable, polite, conducts himself well, does all the right things and is a little shy. The only thing about Michael that's different in private as compared to his public persona is that he loses his shyness when he gets to know people well. He tends to be shy in situations where there are people that are new to him. On our golfing days he never showed such shyness and was in there mixing it with everyone else.

When he went to Newcastle from Real Madrid he still kept a home on the Wirral, so sometimes it was possible for us to resume our golf routine again. He rang me one day, 'Hey Kaiser, I've got a day off on Wednesday, fancy golf with me and my mate Mike Jones?' I'd played with Jonesy before so we all knew each other well. I told Mike that I would be training at City that day so it would have to be an early start if I was going to make it. 'Great,' said Mike. 'I'll book us on at Frodsham for a six-thirty a.m. tee-off.'

I got up at five in order to make sure that I could get over to Frodsham in time for tee-off. I looked out of the bedroom window. It was November, it was cold and it was absolutely chucking it down. It didn't stop raining all the way to Frodsham and though it eased off when I got there the fairways and greens were sodden.

Jonesy had his buggy and Mike was in mine with me driving. Jonesy had hit a nice shot on to the ninth and drove on ahead. He stood just in front of the green near his ball. He was beaming and made-up about his shot. I said to Mike,

'Watch this.' Mike used to like to call me 'Basil Fawlty' and, to be fair, with Mike on board I was having a Basil Fawlty moment in my buggy. I drove straight towards Jonesy as fast as I could. My idea was that I would drive headlong towards him shouting 'Fore' and pull up right in front of him. I obviously hadn't thought this one through. Frodsham golf course has got quite a few hills and dales and it had been raining all night. I was motoring down one of its hills. As I headed towards Jonesy, with Mike hanging on for dear life, I began the shout 'Foooooorrrrrrreeeeeeee' and then as I got closer to Jonesy I slammed on the brakes. The wheels locked, but the buggy carried on going. The fairway was so wet it sent the vehicle on a slide. The expression on Jonesy's face turned from a smile to one of concern to one of absolute terror. As the buggy approached he jumped into the air otherwise he may have ended up underneath it, but despite his jump the buggy whacked his leg with a deadening thud. I watched open-mouthed as Jonesy jumped, hopped and hobbled his way down the fairway for about fifty yards, shouting every form of expletive you could possibly imagine and a few that you probably couldn't. I was horrified. I thought I had broken his leg or bust his tendon or something and I was really concerned.

I looked to Mike for some moral support, but he couldn't speak. He had laughed so hard he had rolled out of the buggy and was now doubled-up on the floor barely able to breathe in between his fits of laughter. So much for moral support from the shy, retiring, sensible Michael Owen. It was one incident with three different reactions. Jonesy, after his outburst, could barely speak through the pain; Michael could barely speak because of the laughter; and I thought it best to keep my mouth shut. What was it that Michael had said about Basil Fawlty?

In the early part of 2009 it was my turn to get hurt. I damaged a tendon in my foot and was out for a while, but the UEFA Cup quarter-final against Hamburg was coming up and I felt that there was a chance that I might be fit in time to play. Mark Bowen, the assistant manager, told me to go up to Newcastle and play with the reserve team about a week before the Hamburg game. Naturally I thought that I had been sent up there to try to get fit in order to give me a chance to play against the German club.

When I got back I bumped into the club secretary. 'I've been at Newcastle,' I said, 'trying to get fit for the Hamburg game.'

He looked sheepish and I sensed that something was wrong. 'You won't be playing against Hamburg, Kaiser,' he said.

'Why?'

'The manager hasn't registered you in the latest UEFA Cup squad list, so you aren't eligible to play.'

I'm not sure whether Mark Bowen knew the situation or not when he sent me to Newcastle, but I do know that the manager did. I just thought that was poor man management. I didn't expect him to give me an explanation as to why I had been excluded, he didn't have to, but I did think that he should have told me.

From that moment nothing was ever the same for me. I went to see Mark Hughes and said, 'I want to carry on playing, if you select me, but if I'm not going to play any part for the rest of the season, I would rather train on my own and look after my injury.'

He was matter of fact and to the point. 'Yes. That's fine,' was all he said. Those were the last words that we spoke.

For the next twelve weeks, I went into training as normal, got changed with the rest of the lads and enjoyed the banter, but then I went to the gym and trained alone. I was available for selection, but I never played for City again. I was number twenty-five in the squad and I think that there was more chance of Mark Hughes putting his boots on and playing than me being picked. Had I been a youngster, maybe I could have gone along with it, but as a senior player I felt that the fact that he didn't tell me I had been removed from the UEFA Cup squad list showed a lack of respect. It was a sad way to end my time at Manchester City, but it was clear that Mark Hughes and I had different views on a lot of things and neither of us was about to change.

I'd had a year of scrapping for survival with Stuart Pearce, a magnificent 'Blue Moon' adventure with Sven and a period of self-imposed solitary under Mark Hughes. After three topsy-turvy years there was no future for me now at City. I collected my things at the end of the season and wondered if things could get any worse.

Things *were* about to take a turn for the worse. I was about to take a gap year.

CHAPTER TWELVE

MANAGER WATCHING

'Insights into The Kaiser's aura, Trapattoni's *cojones* and a jumbo session on a 747'

'Anger and hate are bad advisers.' I used to hear this statement almost every day. In my early days at Bayern Munich the manager Otto Rehhagel coined this phrase. It became his mantra, and the older and more experienced I get the more I understand what he was saying. It's so easy to make decisions when you are angry or you hate a particular situation, but the chances are that you will make bad decisions as your judgement is clouded by intense emotions.

Statements like this are flooding back to me these days as I start to see situations in football and in life from new angles. It's making me realise that I have been a very fortunate accidental apprentice, observing at close quarters some of the best football managers that have ever lived.

I'm not sure that it happens to every player, but there came a time for me where at half-time during a match I'd be trudging up the tunnel and before I'd reached the dressing room I'd already be thinking, 'If I were the manager what would I do now? How would I change things?'

I'd find myself listening intently to the manager's analysis and comparing it with my own. It wasn't something that I was doing so that I could prove I knew more than the manager, I just wanted to see what I had learned and what I could learn. It was like when you do a crossword. If you complete it you feel great, if you don't, you always learn something. So playing 'pretend manager' for me was a no-lose situation. I felt that I could always come out of it a little more knowledgeable.

I started to realise that I'd had an amazing apprenticeship as a footballer. I'd played in great teams and been part of successful international campaigns. I thought about the managers who I had been able to observe at close hand and I really started to reflect on their different styles, attitudes and behaviours. They all had technical knowledge, but they applied it in different ways. That was interesting for me, how they thought about what they wanted to do and the different ways in which they put it across.

I've got to say that when I look back at the managers I've played under, it's a pretty impressive list of names: Beckenbauer, Trapattoni, Rehhagel, Vogts, Riebeck, Voeller, Dalglish, Gullit, Houllier, Benitez, Pearce, Eriksson, Hughes.

Just being in the same room as these people puts you in a pretty special situation. You have a choice. You can just do as you are told and get on with your job; or you can take the opportunity to watch and listen, and learn whether you like what they do or not. As I got a bit older I really enjoyed and appreciated the opportunity to observe these characters, even when I didn't always agree with what they were doing. It was a learning experience of the highest order.

Rudi Voeller was the manager of the German national team from 2000 to 2004. Many people in England will remember him as an irritating, perm-headed, yet very effective forward for Germany, who was prone to mixing it a little. An example of this was in the 1990 World Cup. He was involved in a fracas with the Netherlands' Frank Rijkaard, which saw both of them sent off and Voeller's perm covered in Rijkaard's spit.

As a manager, Voeller had credibility because as a player he had been there and mixed it with the best. During his playing career he won the World Cup in 1990 and was in the final in 1986, as well as winning the Coppa Italia with Roma and the Champions League with Marseille. For me, there was one incident in particular in which he showed that he understood his players, and that players are not machines but individuals.

Voeller knew that I always found it impossible to sleep on planes and that I was not really looking forward to the twelve-hour flight to Japan for the 2002 World Cup. On the plane I found that one by one my teammates drifted off to sleep all around me, so I got up and walked over to the galley where a group of journalists were enjoying a drink. It was a nice atmosphere and as I had a few drinks we found ourselves discussing all sorts of things, not just football. It was a bit like a Saturday night down at your local – a good mix of people, a few drinks, and then a few more, and then you lose track of time. As time passed, I began to notice that a few of the players were beginning to wake up and it slowly dawned on me that I'd actually had quite a bit to drink. I saw the hazy but unmistakable figure of Voeller making his way towards me.

I thought he was going to read me the riot act, but instead he just said, 'Didi, we are landing in two hours; you had better sit down.' I went back to my seat and the hostess arrived and put six glasses of water down in front of me. Voeller had had them sent over. He handled that well. He wasn't mad at me, he just didn't want me falling off the plane when we got to Japan, which I may well have done if he had not intervened when he did.

I appreciated what he had done. He saw me as an individual with my own characteristics, not as a number or as a faceless member of the squad.

I found his handling of that situation really motivated me. As soon as we got to our pre-tournament training camp, I trained extra hard, and I was doing it specifically for him. He showed that he understands the subtle art of how to manage people. We did pretty well under Rudi Voeller in Japan. We reached the final, in which we played against Brazil. So maybe there is something to this idea of acknowledging the person inside the player.

At Bayern Munich I enjoyed my time under the management of an Italian, Giovanni Trapattoni, or 'Trap' as he is known. In fact I had two spells playing under Trap's direction. He came for the 1994/95 season, went back to Italy for a season and then returned to Bayern for a really successful period. We won the Bundesliga and the League Cup double in his first season back, and then went on to win the German Cup the following season. I've got fond memories of Trap's time at Bayern because I also made my debut for the German national team while he was there.

He was fifty-five when he arrived for his second spell in

charge, which to me at the time seemed ancient. But his age was irrelevant, the guy had probably the best managerial CV in the world. In fact he probably still has. He is one of only two managers to have won the league in four different countries and has no less than seven Italian titles with Juventus and Inter Milan. He has won every European competition plus the Intercontinental Cup, and holds the record for UEFA Cup wins – two with Juventus and one with Milan. That's not to mention his glittering playing career for AC Milan, which included two European Cup wins.

He was a greying, middle-aged man who was beginning to bulk out a bit. He tried hard with the German language, but would often find himself getting tongue-tied and mixed up, so there was a lot of unintentional comedy. What came through clearly though was that he was a very nice, likeable man who cared about people. Behind that though, was a man who knew how to win silverware on a scale that nobody had ever done before.

This was Giovanni Trapattoni, a legend. I was determined that I was going to listen carefully to this fella, because something about what he knew and the way he applied it led to success time after time. I was hoping that some of his magic dust would rub off on me.

He stands out as a manager that I will try to emulate in many ways, because I liked a lot of what I saw him do. Trap was meticulous in his organisation and planning, a characteristic that I have seen since in other great managers. He worked hard with players on positioning and thinking about the game. I think Trap was a big influence on my game, because I was not known for tearing about all over the place.

I was known for thinking about where I should be and trying to make sure that I was there at the right time. Essentially, I built a fulfilling career out of the foundations that Trap laid down for me. His investment in people was genuine and not for his own personal glorification.

There was a little incident that I will always remember. In a way it was nothing really, but it is something that I will never forget because it summed up his hard-working, unselfish ethos.

Training had finished over an hour ago, and I was about to drive away from the training ground with another Bayern player when I heard voices out on one of the pitches. Trap was still out there. We had a fringe player, a good lad, but it was pretty clear that he wasn't going to break through at Bayern. Trap, one of the greatest coaches in the world, had this lad out there doing extra work one-to-one, working on his weaker left foot. We knew that the lad wouldn't make it with the team. Trap knew it too, but session after session he would work with this player on his left foot. Trap was right at the top of the tree. His interest was not in his own personal gain but in trying to help this player because he thought that was the right thing to do. I liked that a lot.

Everybody loved Trap because he spent so much time with the young players and the players who were not even going to make it. He made every player in the first team feel that their contribution was valued. I found working with him a great experience, he was exceptional.

One thing I do think about when I look back on my time with him, is that I would have loved the chance to work with him in his native language, or for him to have had a better mastery of German. When he first came to Munich he used an interpreter. This worked reasonably well except that Trap was notorious for his long training sessions, sometimes they went on for two and a half hours. Part of his formula for success was attention to detail, in particular team shape and positioning, and he would go over and over these things until he was happy. Having an interpreter translate these very precise points of detail could take an age, and the sessions could go on even longer than normal. Also, I always felt that Trap's interpreter was a bit 'busy'. He had his own thoughts on the game, even though he was just an interpreter, and sometimes I would wonder if he was relaying Trap's opinions or his version of Trap's opinions.

Trap tried hard to master the German language, to everyone's amusement, most especially the press. He was the Yogi Berra of German football and the press were always keen to hear another one of his 'Trapisms'. In a stilted German accent he would say things like, 'Don't say cat until you have got it in the bag.' Once when referring to a particular player he said he was 'Weak like a bottle empty'. He was hilarious, without meaning to be, and the press couldn't get enough of it.

There was one 'Trapism' that the press didn't pick up on. We had lost a game and performed poorly into the bargain. Trap felt that we had let the Bayern fans down with our performance. Back at the training ground, with just two days before the next match, he called everybody over into the centre circle and told us all to sit down. He walked about in the middle, composing himself like a general, thinking about what he was going to try to put over to us in his stilted and limited German. He began, 'We a getta sticka now. But eet too late. We not now go to fans and say "Fans, we are veery sorry." Instead, we hava to do it on the peetch.' This style of talking tickled some of the lads and you could see the smirks and smiles being forcibly held back on a number of faces. We all tried to show due respect to this serious situation.

Pausing to look around the group he began what was going to be his call to arms. 'In two days, we play at home. Then we have to show the fans that we have got . . . that we have . . . that we . . .' He was struggling to find a word. What was it that we had to show the fans that we had? The word wasn't coming and so he firmly placed a hand over his crotch and pulled at his testicles and said triumphantly 'Cojones'. Then he realised that this was a Spanish word and that he was trying to speak in German.

Looking for help he gestured in the direction of Giovane Elber, our Brazilian striker, who of course was familiar with this word because it is the same in Portuguese. Trap tugged at his 'cojones' and said to Giovane, 'What are these things called in German?'

Giovane didn't hesitate with his reply, right away he said 'Mushi'.

Everybody looked at Giovane, some in surprise, others trying to stifle their laughter. 'Mushi' in German is 'fanny' in English. Trap was unaware of the reactions of the players because he was rehearsing in his mind how to deliver this sentence properly now that he had the word that he had so badly needed to complete it.

So Trap is now like a poet, pacing the centre circle, getting his lines right. 'Yes. Yes. In two days time we must get out there and show the fans that we have a fanny.' Players were now aching with the pain of holding in their laughter and trying not to smile. Many were pulling their shirts over their mouths, but there was no stopping Trap now he was on a roll. 'We are going to say "look we got fanny".' Now, it was only a matter of time before someone erupted. But Trap just would not stop. 'Fanny, fanny, fanny, that's what I want.'

Sides were splitting and it was inevitable that someone broke into uncontrollable laughter. The moment that happened everybody just let loose. The centre circle was a ring of hilarity with players falling sideways laughing, banging the floor to try to control their mirth and in some cases wiping away the tears of laughter.

As we calmed down and order was restored, it was clear that Trap was not amused. He was furious. Here he was trying to get us to earn back the respect of the fans and we were rolling about laughing. He just could not fathom what was going on. He glared around the centre circle. 'Stop. Stop. All of you. What you are laughing?'

Sheepishly, Giovane explained the joke and apologised for being an idiot. Trap let this sink in for a moment. You could see him thinking back over what he had said. This time in his mind he was substituting 'fanny' every time he thought he had said the German word for 'cojones'. First there was a little smile, then his smile widened and suddenly Trap burst into a fit of hysterical laughter as what he had been saying and why we had been laughing sank in. This time we all laughed with him and he liked that.

Trap already had everyone's respect because of the way he was with people and what he had done in the game. I think that little 'cojones' episode, and others like it, earned Trap extra respect. They helped people to see him as a normal guy, a nice fella, who had that invaluable ability to be able to laugh at himself. Some managers believe that you have to appear infallible, but that's when they become distant and unapproachable. Trap believed the opposite. He knew that he was as capable as all of us of occasionally making a fool of himself, but he embraced it and relished it. He could laugh at himself and players loved him for it. Whoever it was that said 'The leadership instinct you are born with is backbone. You develop the funny bone and the wishbone that go with it' must have been thinking of Trap. Leadership was in his bones – his backbone, funny bone and wishbone.

Erich Ribbeck, whom I played under with the German national team, was another manager who had an interesting way of dealing with foreign words that he could not pronounce or remember. He simply substituted an image that he thought might be appropriate. We were playing Northern Ireland and about three hours before the game he called us to a prematch meeting to go over the opposition and clarify our tactics. On a big white board he began writing up the names of the Northern Ireland players – Wright, Nolan, Taggart, Hill, Hunter, Horlock, Morrow, Lomas – then he had to stop. He was racking his brains for the name of the big Northern Ireland centre forward. It wouldn't come to him. In frustration he wrote 'Ochse'. Everybody laughed as they instantly under-stood who he was referring to. 'Ochse' is the German word for 'ox'. Clearly Erich couldn't remember the centre forward's name but had an image of him in his mind as a big, beefy, animal-type. It was Ian Dowie, who forever after was referred to in the German changing room as 'Ochse'.

Before Trap we enjoyed two stints at Bayern under the leadership of the resident 'firefighter' Franz Beckenbauer. Whenever there was a problem at Bayern, The Kaiser would come in reluctantly to steady the ship. I think that he had decided that he had given up on management after he won the 1990 World Cup as manager of the West German team and then had a season in France managing Marseille. I think he felt he wanted to move on to other things, but he was Bayern through and through. Having played 427 games for the club, whenever there was a crisis that needed a safe pair of hands for a while The Kaiser got the call. When it came to Bayern, much as he may have wanted to, he just couldn't say 'No'.

So he took over the first time about halfway through the season in 1994. It was lucky for me that he did, because he saw something in me that the previous manager didn't and really gave me a run in the team. This kicked off my whole career.

It's nice when people in England refer to me as Kaiser, it's a nickname that has followed me around and I like it. But if you are German there is only one Kaiser, and that is Franz Beckenbauer.

He had his own style of management. I think this was due to a combination of two factors – he had achieved at the highest level and he was relaxed because he felt his future lay elsewhere other than managing Bayern Munich. He is not just a German legend, he is up there in that elite list of the greatest players of all time. As a result, and I'm not sure that he is even aware of it, he carries an aura around him. You can feel it the moment he walks into a room. That's a great asset that not everybody has, but it means he commands a room and people's attention gravitates towards him.

His relaxed style had the effect of introducing a little reverse psychology. When he first took over as manager The Kaiser changed the training schedule so that we started early at 9.30 a.m. It was a surprise to some players, who preferred things the way they were before. There was a simple reason for this change: The Kaiser lived some way out of Munich; he liked his golf; so he wanted to be back home and on the first tee at 2 p.m. every day.

One of the players, unhappy with this new regime, thought he would test out whether there was any leeway. He asked the boss, 'When are we next in?' He was hoping to hear that perhaps this new regime was temporary and that we would go back to a 10.30 a.m. start.

The Kaiser was quite matter of fact about it, almost jaunty. He just said, 'If you don't want to come in don't bother. It's your career and it's your life. It's optional.' With that he walked off to make his way home and play his golf. This got people thinking about what he could possibly have meant by saying 'It's optional'.

Of course what he meant was that 'if you don't turn up when I tell you to then don't expect to be selected to play'. Despite what he said about it being optional, in a funny way it left the players in no doubt that training started at 9.30 a.m. every day and if you wanted to be included in his plans you had better be there. There was nothing optional about it.

As I said, it was a kind of reverse psychology. I know that I made sure I got there extra early just so that he knew that

I had no doubts in my mind about where I wanted to be and where I was going. The amazing thing about The Kaiser and his aura was that he didn't need a rule book, everything was 'optional'. His aura seemed to let you know that if you knew what was good for your career you fell in with The Kaiser's preferred option.

Every manager has his own style. The things that have happened to me have helped to shape my thinking about what my style might be like, should I make it as a manager. You can learn from things that you do like and you can learn from the things that you don't like. In the management stakes to date I have achieved sweet FA, so I hold my hands up on that score. Mark Hughes, who was one of my managers at Manchester City, has achieved quite a lot, so his methods must work. For me though, I wasn't keen on his style of management. Though there is no disputing the fact that Hughes has achieved great things, primarily on a limited budget, so fair play to him.

Mark's methods are tried and tested and I learned a lot about management by watching him. I learned how I don't want to do it. That sounds strange, because he came with a great track record and all of the Blackburn players said good things about him. Clearly his methods work for him, but for me he was too distant. All managers have to put some distance between themselves and the players, but Hughes, I think, took that too far. There was one occasion when we went on the train to London for an away match. Hughes and his backroom team had a separate carriage; we got on the team coach at Euston and they had their own minibus; then after breakfast on match day, they went for a walk in one direction and we went in the other. I didn't like that. It was as if there were two separate camps – them and us.

I remember that we lost a game that we should have won against bottom-of-the-table West Brom. Hughes stormed about the dressing room and read us the riot act, which he was quite entitled to do. Then he shouted, 'We are all in this together.'

I bit my lip because I wanted to say, 'That comes as news to me.' I kept quiet and so did everyone else. There was a resounding silence in the dressing room. I think that silence was significant. I think it told the real story.

Then of course there was Sven-Goran Eriksson. A man of such charm and sophistication that had James Bond been Swedish the character would surely have been modelled upon him. He had everything. He was polished, professional, genuinely charming, polite, dapper, unflappable and likeable. Added to that he had a great knowledge of the game and was prepared to show himself as a leader.

One thing I will take from Sven is that come rain, hail or shine, he is always, and I mean always, the first person out on the training pitch. Training began at 10.30 a.m. and you could set your watch by it. Sven would be standing there at 10.20 a.m. precisely, waiting for everybody to arrive. Nobody ever got on to the training pitch before Sven. There are some managers these days that don't go near the training pitch. Some would argue that you don't need to with the level of coaches and technical staff now on call at the big clubs. But that's not the issue. I believe that Sven was making a point about leadership and togetherness by being first out there every day. It's true, he didn't have to be there, he chose to be there. As a result, I'd say that when Sven was at Manchester City we definitely punched above our weight. If Sven had said 'We are all in this together' you can bet your bottom dollar that, to a man, everyone in that squad would have been right by his side. He was one of us, yet we knew he was the boss. He cared about us, but he wasn't soft. He led from the front and made us want to play for him.

As far as my time at Liverpool is concerned, people may think that Rafa broke my heart. He was in charge when I left Liverpool, but I could have stayed. It wasn't down to Rafa that I left. He just told me the situation as it was. Had I stayed I would have been a bit-part player. I couldn't allow my Anfield career to peter out and end with a whimper, it meant far too much to me. So it wasn't that Rafa broke my heart, it was that I wanted to leave Liverpool in a dignified manner so that people would have good memories of me.

Even if Rafa had forcibly removed me from Anfield, which he didn't, there is no doubt in my mind that he would still be near the top of my managerial Christmas card list. Remember, throughout my career I've been coached by some of the best managers and coaches in the world, yet it seemed like every week Rafa would come up with yet another unique insight into a situation that I had never heard before. Sometimes talking to Rafa was a little like when you go out to your car on a winter's morning and the windscreen's iced up. You can't see anything so you switch on the de-icer. Gradually you start to see through the impenetrable barrier of ice, a hazy picture emerges as the ice melts and then within about two minutes you have a full technicolour image before your very eyes. Rafa had the ability to achieve this rapid transformation from total blankness to incredible insight in just two minutes, whether it was about the overall approach to a match or a tiny little situation in a game. He was incisive. He had the mind of a prosecution barrister and the words of a Spanish troubadour.

I still have the debate with some of the Liverpool lads today. In my mind Rafa is pure managerial genius. Some of the lads, though acknowledging his capabilities, won't go that far. He is quite unemotional though and he's not big on relationships. Stevie Gerrard and I have had quite intense discussions about this. Stevie's view was, 'He never praises you.' Not that Stevie was the kind of guy who needed praise, but I think he thought that it might help some of the other players if they got some positive strokes. I said that the greatest praise that you can receive from a manager is to be picked to play in the team, and I always regarded that as high praise. But I think from a captain's perspective, Stevie would have liked to have had a stronger relationship with the manager. Rafa's lack of emotion contrasted with Stevie, who is a very passionate guy. Maybe he didn't tick all the boxes for Stevie. But I repeat, tactically this man is the major dude. Pure genius.

When Rafa had a not-so-successful spell in Milan he came back to the Wirral, where he still has a family home. As I was starting to think about a career in management I rang him up for a chat. He invited me over for lunch, an invitation that I gratefully accepted. We talked about football, or rather he talked and I sat and listened in awe. It was master and pupil. He moved salt and pepper pots here and there across the table as he enthusiastically explained how it is possible to beat Barcelona. My only disappointment was that all too soon it was over. On the way home I recalled the time after the Champions League final when I had sat in front of Rafa having not slept for the best part of thirty-six hours. I was so engrossed in what he was saying – his thoughts, his ideas, his clever incisiveness – that I would gladly have sat there listening for another thirty-six hours.

Managers see things from a range of perspectives and some place more emphasis on one thing than another, probably depending on what they have seen work in the past. The really successful managers have an intuitive understanding of the things that you need to put in place to: one – make people feel comfortable and valued; and two – to really motivate people to achieve. This idea that there are two sets of factors that managers should be aware of to get the best from their people ironically had its origins about ten miles north of my hometown of Munich at the Dachau Concentration Camp at the end of the Second World War. An American psychologist, Frederick Herzberg, who had enlisted as a US Army patrol sergeant, was one of the first to witness the horrific scenes at the camp. In due course his observations at the liberation of Dachau helped him to develop a theory called the motivation-hygiene theory. It talks about managers satisfying two distinct sets of needs if they are to get the best from their people. Things like relationships, working conditions, pay, status and security are the essential elements, 'the hygiene factors', that have to be in place to have any chance of achieving anything. However, high performance will only come from addressing 'the motivational factors'. Examples of these are constant achievement, recognition, the quality of work that you do, being given responsibility and the prospects for advancement. The lesson I draw from this is that the motivational factors only have a significant effect if the hygiene factors are in place first, and if all you offer is hygiene factors don't expect to have a high-performing team.

As Sven-Goran Eriksson demonstrated so brilliantly, with his emphasis on relationships and making everybody feel wanted and valued, if you lay down a good foundation of hygiene factors and add motivational factors as he did, suddenly you get people punching above their weight. As I think we did during his season at Manchester City.

Relationships can be tricky, especially with the mix of characters and egos that you get in a dressing room. I believe that concentrating on these is a big part of being a good football manager, because if you don't and you start shouting 'We are all in this together' you may well be met with an overwhelming silence.

I like the way Herzberg has of looking at these things because it definitely rings true for me from my days at Bayern Munich. I had the five-year contract, the salary, the security, the good working environment and so on. All the hygiene factors were in place, yet I didn't feel properly recognised or that I was in a position of responsibility. I felt that I was still treated as the kid that came through the ranks. I didn't think that the necessary motivational factors were there for me and that's when I started to feel that I would like to move on.

Management is a fascinating field in which you never stop learning. As I begin to think about my future, these amazing experiences with top managers will be times that I will continue to look back on and learn from.

I'm really fortunate, too, to have the opportunity to go and sit in the presence of people like Rafa while they hold court on the art of the manager. He can thrill me with the finest detail of a single play to a well-argued theory on how to beat Barcelona. For now, beating Barcelona is nothing more than an interesting and fanciful idea. I have to earn the right to be called 'gaffer'.

CHAPTER THIRTEEN

THE GAP YEAR

'When you walk through a storm . . .'

I was in a dark place. A very dark place. Then the Australian cricket team had a dramatic batting collapse. It caused something to happen that gave me a dramatic wake-up call. It was time to move back into the light.

There's an old saying that I like: 'It's not how far you fall, it's how high you bounce.' It's a very fortunate man who has a life that is blemish-free, in which there are precious few disappointments and where relationships are smooth. Who in life will not make mistakes and misjudgements?

As I prepare myself for what I hope will be a long career as a football manager, I'm glad that I can reflect on my gap year. It followed on from the most difficult and painful year of my life. It was tough, it was traumatic and at times it was chaotic. For a time I was lost. I think a good manager has to understand that people aren't always perfect, even people who have a cupboard full of medals can lose their direction sometimes.

DIETMAR HAMANN

You have to have been there to fully understand what happens when the wheels come off and what you can do about it.

Believe me, I've been there. The wheels came off good and proper and dealing with the situations that emerged have made me a better person. I understand myself more and I think I'll be able to understand other people better as a result.

I am a natural optimist and always feel that every cloud has a silver lining. The situation I found myself in was less of a cloud and more of a tropical storm. The upside was that the lining turned out not to be silver, but solid gold. Her name is Liz Robinson and everything in my life has been on an upward trajectory since the moment we met.

What I've learned to appreciate is that the structures that act as the scaffolding holding up our day-to-day lives can be very fragile. When the scaffolding comes crashing down our weaknesses can come to the fore. That's why I think it's essential that managers look at the whole person when they are dealing with players rather than instructing pieces of meat as to where to stand and when to run.

One major change in your life can be difficult to deal with. When two or three or four major things happen at about the same time you can find yourself in a maelstrom.

As my time at Liverpool was coming to a close, my marriage was going through a difficult patch. These things happen. People grow apart and their perspective can change. That's what happened with us and while I was becoming more engrossed in a new life in England my wife wasn't as keen. She wanted to take the children back to Germany. I was and still am very close to my kids. I tried to drop them off at school before training as often as I could. They meant more to me than anything and the thought of them being taken away was something that I could not bear to contemplate. One of the reasons behind my decision not to go to Bolton was that I felt a move to Manchester might result in a change of heart and I could rescue the situation.

So I'd left the club of my dreams, I was in a new house in a new neighbourhood and playing for a new team. Added to this, the prospect of what I saw as losing my children was playing on my mind constantly. All of this newness and the possibility of the unthinkable happening was shaking the scaffolding that held my life together.

Eventually it happened. My wife took the momentous decision to take the kids back to Germany and there was nothing I could do about it. I was still under contract at Manchester City and suddenly the rug had been pulled from under my feet. I was devastated.

It felt horrible. As if someone had turned all the lights out. My kids were such an important part of my life and now I could only get to see them when I was able to jump on an aeroplane to Munich. I was in turmoil. I couldn't sit there staring at the walls of the house. I needed to fill the time. I needed to switch off all of the thoughts that were swirling around in my head. A lot of times I just didn't want to think. It was too painful.

I began to drink more than is healthy for a footballer. What man doesn't when his marriage falls apart and his children are separated from him? Then I turned to something that kept my brain occupied and supplied a bit of an adrenalin rush. My liking for a wager was becoming a bit more than just a recreational pastime. At that time anything was better than thinking about my situation.

When I was in Germany I would go with a friend who had horses to watch the carriage racing. I liked it – the atmosphere, the day out, it was great. While at Liverpool I would go to the track with Robbie Fowler and some of the other lads because Robbie owned some racehorses. I used to bet modestly and for fun. I suppose if you are good with words you do crosswords. I'm good with numbers and I love sport, so betting was a perfect combination for me.

Of course now you can bet on anything, and spread betting adds some spice to it because it requires more thought to be given to probabilities and enables you to make calculations about the level of risk that you are prepared to take. For me it was the more numbers the better, the more probabilities and possibilities, the more my brain was engaged and the less I thought about the devastation that was going on inside of me.

I was having a hard time sleeping at night. In fact it became almost impossible for me to sleep.

I'd become very interested in cricket. When I met Freddie Flintoff he began to explain the rules of the game and how it worked. He even took me for some instruction in the nets and I was hooked on the game. I watched it more and more on the TV and of course it was made even more interesting if Freddie was playing. Sitting there alone at nights I was grateful for the cricket. If there was a match on somewhere in the world I could stay up and watch it because sleep was something I couldn't do.

I guess I hadn't realised it, but the spread bets I had started to do were becoming more risky and more bizarre. Sometimes I would win, sometimes I would lose, but that wasn't the point. These things creep up on you as you build a resilience to risk and it just became an exercise in trying to numb the pain I was feeling.

It was a little like playing the stock market really. I held an account with the balance adjusted upwards or downwards at the end of each day.

Then one night there was a test match in Australia. The Aussies were playing South Africa so I bought Australia for £2,800 at 340 runs. That means for every run over 340 you win £2,800 and for every run under you lose that amount. If Australia could hit 400 I'd get £168,000 just for watching a cricket match when I couldn't sleep anyway. In my confused state that seemed somehow logical at the time.

When you are in that position every boundary is a joy and every wicket feels like a stab in the heart. By the end of the night I felt like I had been scalped. The Australians collapsed for 237. That's a number I remember well. It cost me £288,400.

The rest of the night was spent trying, against the odds, to get some sleep. When I got up the next day I had to go into training at Manchester City. I looked at the mess that was me in the mirror. 'Didi,' I said, 'things have got to change.'

I was struggling through that final season at City, and then I had the good fortune to meet Liz. Here was someone who could understand my eccentricities and was fun to be around, yet she could also be disciplined and businesslike when she needed to be. She demanded discipline and focus from me. She saved me from myself and helped me to rebuild the scaffolding around my life. She gave me a reason to get up in the morning and to go to bed at night. When it was clear that I wasn't going to get another contract extension at City we decided that I should have a gap year, get myself together again and plot the route towards getting my FA coaching badges.

Over the years I heard the Kop singing the Liverpool anthem 'You'll Never Walk Alone' literally hundreds and hundreds of times. People sing the words without even thinking about them. It's an amazing feeling when you are out there at Anfield and the Kop get into full swing with that song, it's one of the greatest experiences in world sport. It can make the hairs on the back of your neck stand up and give you goosebumps. After getting through a very dark period in my life I appreciate that song even more. People should listen to those words. Thank God that at the end of the road there was a golden sun in the form of Liz. She arrived in my life just at the right time like the sweet silver song of the lark.

So as I say, it's not how far you fall it's how high you bounce. My gap year allowed me some time to get ready to bounce.

I would have liked another year at Manchester City, but under Mark Hughes that was never going to happen. I was thirty-five going on thirty-six when my contract expired. There was a loose enquiry from Queens Park Rangers followed by a short discussion, but it didn't go anywhere. Other than that there was not much interest in a senior professional who was not quite past his sell-by date. I was beginning to accept that nothing lasts for ever, especially a career in football, and that it was time to move on.

I started to do my coaching badges. I went on a ten-day residential course with the likes of Andy Cole, Shefki Kuqi, Kevin Davies and Danny Mills. Then I agreed with Kenny Dalglish that I would do my practical hours at Liverpool's academy.

The first part of the course is pretty basic, but to be fair you need to do the basics. As a top footballer you get everything laid on for you, so putting out cones and making sure there were enough bibs is something I'd never had to think about. I hadn't laid out a bib since my children first started eating solids.

The sessions get progressively more detailed, looking at things such as nutrition, fitness, trends in football and tactics. Nothing was new to me, but it was good to debate things with others because there is no one right answer in football. Different people have different views. I passed the A Licence and now the next step for me is to go on to the Pro Licence, which is more about the management side of things such as handling the press and reporting to the board.

I was keeping myself reasonably fit and thinking that after a season out of the game now was the time to start having a look for opportunities in coaching. I didn't have to look far. A friend of mine lives next door to Karl Robinson in Liverpool. Karl was a coach at the Liverpool academy when I was a Liverpool player. He subsequently became Paul Ince's assistant at MK Dons and took the manager's position when Incey moved on after his second spell in charge. He was the youngest manager in the Football League at the age of just twenty-nine.

Anyway, my pal got into a neighbourly chat with Karl and was asking him how things were going at MK Dons. Karl said, 'Well, I really need a good holding midfield player.' Even though I'd not played for over a year my name came up and Karl duly gave me a call.

'Kaiser, do you fancy coming to MK Dons?'

I was a bit surprised at this and I said, 'What as?'

I was even more surprised at his answer. 'I want you to come as a player.'

I didn't want to go backwards. I'd decided what direction my life was going to take and being a journeyman player wasn't the way I wanted to go. Coaching was to be my future, so I said 'I'll come but only if I can coach. I'm happy to play but the most important thing is getting the opportunity to coach.'

Karl agreed and I set about getting myself fit after a one-year layoff. It wasn't as hard as you might expect, because one thing made it much easier than it should have been – I wanted to do it. I wanted to get my fitness back and start firing on all cylinders again. When you are highly motivated to do something, everything is much easier.

Karl had brought in the experienced Scottish former England coach John Gorman. I thought this was a good opportunity to learn the coaching ropes from someone who been there on the front line. Alongside him was another Scot, Alex Rae, who had also worked under Paul Ince. So I got stuck in with bibs and cones, drills and routines, and offered advice whenever I thought it could be useful.

I made my debut in the first game of the season away against Walsall, with the M6 motorway almost on the goal line and a crowd of 4,043. It was a different experience to what I had been used to, but it made me realise something. It doesn't matter what level of football you are playing at, as long as you are winning it's a great feeling. We won 2–1 and I came away feeling very content.

I enjoyed being out on the pitch, trying to help the lads by passing on some of the things that I had learnt about positioning and shape from the likes of Trap and Rafa. With the season progressing we were knocking on the door for the play-off spots, and I like to think that I was making a contribution on and off the pitch.

It was off the pitch where I was now interested in making the biggest impact. When Alex Rae left to join Paul Ince again, this time as his assistant at Notts County, I had a word with Karl. There was a young midfielder at MK Dons who was a very good player, but he wasn't getting enough game time. Often if I was in the team it meant that he was out of it. So I suggested to Karl that with Alex gone he should give this lad more games and let me concentrate more on coaching, which we agreed.

I didn't realise it at the time but this signalled my last game for MK Dons. We went to Tranmere Rovers and lost 4–2. The match was memorable for the performance of a young man called Dale Jennings, who scored two goals for the home team in the first twenty-five minutes.

Eight months or so later I was asked to go to speak to Dale Jennings, who became involved in what was described as the most remarkable transfer of 2011. Dale, who had been at Liverpool for six years as a youngster, had played only twenty-nine competitive games for Tranmere Rovers when another of my former clubs, Bayern Munich, made an audacious bid for him. The clubs reached a deal worth £500,000, which could rise to £1.8 million with add-ons.

I got a call from Bayern's director of sport, Christian Nerlinger, he put me in the picture and explained that the lad was having some reservations about moving to Germany. He asked if I could go and have a chat with him. I was glad to do it. I sat down with Dale, who seemed a quiet, reserved sort of lad. I explained to him that this was a great opportunity, not only to learn about football in the great Bayern tradition in the way that I had, but to sample a new culture. I told him what a great thing it had been for me to come to England and see and try different things and that opportunities like this had to be grasped with both hands. I said, 'You need to get out there and make sure that you learn the language. A lot of English players struggle to settle abroad because they struggle with the language.'

I reported back to Christian. Having seen the lad play and now talked to him, I felt that as long as Bayern could put a strong and stable support network around him to help him to settle, then they had got a prospect on their hands.

I wasn't there to try to persuade Dale to go, only to help him to think it through properly. Some weeks later he signed, which was tremendous business for Tranmere Rovers and an amazing opportunity for a Liverpool lad in Munich. If his time there is half as successful as this Munich lad's time was in Liverpool, then he's got a great career ahead of him. For now, he will have to knuckle down in the Bayern second team and I'll be watching with interest.

Meanwhile, Derek Fazackerley, who had been the assistant manager at Manchester City, had gone to be Sven-Goran Eriksson's assistant at Leicester City. I'd always kept in touch with Faz. We spoke every so often on the phone and just kept up with who was doing what and who might go where. In January 2011 I was on the phone to Faz. He told me that Chris Powell, one of the Leicester City coaches, had got the manager's job at Charlton, which was a great move for him. I said, 'Who's taking over from him?'

Faz was quite casual, he replied, 'Why don't you come into the club and we can have a chat about it?'

I went to Leicester and met with Faz and Sven. It felt really good to be in their presence again. After chatting for ages about all sorts of stuff, including Sven's plans for Leicester, we got round to talking about the vacant coaching position. Sven piped up, 'If you want to come it's yours.' It was as simple as that. It was a higher league, a chance to concentrate on coaching and to do it with two people that I had a great deal of respect for. It was a hard decision, but I really felt that this was an opportunity.

It was a new year and a new coaching challenge but one thing remained the same – the charismatic and charming Sven. Myself and a few of the other backroom staff were sitting around in a room one day and Sven spotted the youth-team coach. He looked over at him and in his relaxed and undulating Swedish accent said, 'The young man I asked you to give a trial, did he come in?' The coach assured him that he had been. 'Good,' said Sven. 'I was buying my railway ticket at the station and the lady behind the counter was very pretty. She said, "Mr Eriksson, can you fix up a trial for my son? He's a very good footballer." I said I could so she gave me her phone number. Yes, a very pretty lady.' And with that he walked off.

I said to the youth-team coach, 'Was the lad any good?'

'He was OK but he wasn't a youth, he was nineteen, I couldn't do anything for him.' Sven's desire to please a pretty lady sometimes knows no bounds.

In just one season I'd gone from gap-year dropout to getting some coaching experience at two different clubs. This was a great way to find my feet, but gradually something began to dawn on me.

I've noticed that some people make very good number twos. Most successful managers, politicians and business leaders have had unsung heroes standing next to them. Sven took all the headlines but he always had Tord Grip by his side. Clough and Taylor, Shankly and Paisley, Paisley and Fagan are other examples, and so I could go on.

Being a good number two is a delicate art and it's an invaluable role. The thing I had learnt from my time at MK Dons and Leicester City was that, at this stage of my career at any rate, being a number two is not what I want.

Of course it was great to be around Sven, and although I wasn't his number two I would get asked my opinion sometimes on team issues. From time to time I would make suggestions about what we should do as regards tactics or team selection. Sometimes he would take my ideas on board and sometimes he wouldn't. That's fair enough because the buck stopped with him. If the team didn't deliver the goods then his head was on the block.

So I had no problems with him doing that. It just helped me to realise something about myself. I'd planned to ease my way into management by getting some coaching experience for a couple of years first. As I started coaching I found that I was bursting with thoughts, ideas and opinions on how the game should be played, and it left me feeling a little frustrated and unfulfilled if they were not taken on board. The art of a good number two is not to feel this way, to be more accepting and tolerant and to sit comfortably as an adviser. I was finding it difficult to apply this art all of the time, but felt that it was something I must try to do as part of my development.

When Paul Hart left Swindon Town my name somehow got into the frame for the vacant manager's job. I was asked to go and meet the directors for an interview. I think they had a shortlist of maybe five people, and then, according to the papers, they narrowed it down to just two names – mine and former West Ham United flair player, Paolo di Canio.

Until I went for that interview I hadn't realised quite how much I wanted to be a manager sooner than I had planned. Talking to the Swindon Town directors really whetted my appetite for putting a team together and playing my way. We had a great discussion about budgets, the players and how I might shape things. As I came away from the meeting I real-ised that I really, really wanted the job, much more than I expected to. I went down to Swindon thinking 'Well, this is going to be good interview practice' and I came away so fired up that I wanted it.

I waited anxiously for a call. They were taking their time over the decision and some of the press were speculating that I was going to get the nod over Paolo di Canio. When the call came they told me the news that Paolo had been offered the job and he had accepted. I was well gutted.

I had been imagining it all in my mind – how I would work in training, looking at the shape of the team, thinking about who would make a good backroom team. So when the news came it was a big disappointment. I didn't expect to feel that way at all, I thought that I would just be able to view it as welcome practice for when I was ready to go after my first management position. Suddenly, being a manager in a few years' time seemed less appealing. I was feeling that I wanted it, and more than that, I wanted it now.

There was only one thing for it. I applied Houllier's rule of allowing myself two minutes of disappointment and then I started to look to the future. I still had a job at Leicester City working with great people, but this episode had helped me to realise that I couldn't wait two, three or four years to try my hand at management. I felt ready to take on a challenge now.

I was enjoying the close season so much more than in the gap year. I had a chance to play more cricket and took my batting record up to three runs. Also I was involved with Sven in his search for new players. We had something like eleven lads going out of contract at Leicester City so there was some squad rebuilding to be done.

It was a great summer, I felt really alive again.

Just as I was about to head back to Leicester for preseason training the phone rang.

Opportunity had knocked.

CHAPTER FOURTEEN

STOCKPORT, SO GOOD THEY NAMED IT ONCE

'Over the moon with eight players, no stadium and training at the farm'

It took just sixteen seconds for the Stockport County squad – all eight of them – to introduce themselves. Three were left over from the previous season's disastrous League Two relegation and five were signed by former manager Ray Mathias. I wasn't slow on the uptake. I knew from my previous experience that football teams comprised eleven players. So that was item one on my agenda.

But hey, what was exciting was that I was a manager and I had my own agenda. I was master of my own destiny. The buck stopped here. I knew that taking the manager's job at Stockport County was a big, big risk, but I weighed it up and decided that it was a risk worth taking. In my excitement it hadn't quite registered what a big task I had taken on.

Once again, the approach came right out of the blue. Stockport had endured a complicated series of ownership issues over recent years and there was talk that a new consortium was about to come in and take over. I got a call from a friend of mine in Liverpool who knew Tony Evans who was leading a consortium of investors led by personal-injury lawyers GT Law. 'All right Kaiser?' he said. 'It looks like Tony's going to get a deal done at Stockport and I've mentioned to him that you'd make a good manager. Do you want to talk to him?'

I was intrigued. But football is a game of intrigue, and there are always stories about this takeover going through and that job coming up and more often than not they are media rumours. So I said, 'I'll have a chat, but until it gets to an advanced stage I can't commit one way or the other.'

I met Tony soon afterwards. He's a big Liverpool fan so we immediately had some common ground. He outlined how the takeover was going to work and the budgets that would be available. At any level a key to your success is having a decent budget to start with, it's then a matter of how you spend it. I talked to Tony about my ideas of management and in particular I remembered when Rafa first came into Liverpool and created a very small close-knit group. A small backroom team at Stockport would be essential anyway, but I genuinely felt that it was the right approach. I said it would be essential to have an excellent fitness coach and a strong assistant manager.

It was a good meeting and I was beginning to warm to the idea, but as far as I was concerned it was all 'in theory'. Takeovers are difficult to complete and there was not long to go before preseason training was due to start. All sorts of things could go wrong with due diligence and personality clashes not to mention whether the money would materialise when it was supposed to, which is something that happens quite frequently in proposed takeovers.

With all of these variables up in the air, I told Tony, 'I'm very interested, but until you are sure that this is definitely going to go through there is nothing more to talk about. If you contact me when you have done the deal I will give you a straight decision then. Just keep me in the loop.'

There was no news and I went back to Leicester City. Preseason was just over a week away and then the phone rang. I got that call. It was Tony saying that the takeover was going through and the job was mine if I wanted it. I told him that he would have to speak to Leicester City and ask their permission to make a formal approach and then I could give him an answer.

Tony spoke to Leicester and the next thing I knew Sven was on the phone. His accent undulated more than ever as he tried to visualise where Stockport was. 'Kaiser. What is this? Stockport? Where is Stockport?' I expected him to say 'go ahead', but he clearly had his reservations. He carried on. 'Kaiser, when did you finish playing? It's early for you yet. You should wait. I think you are going in too low, you can do bigger things.'

This was not the encouragement I was expecting, but he finished his pitch by saying, 'Look, speak to them by all means, but I want you to know that I don't want you to go.'

After I had started to get excited about going to Stockport, Sven had put doubts in my mind. Should I stay or should I go? I went to meet Tony again and sought assurances about the things we had agreed. There was also an incumbent manager and I wanted that situation to be dealt with properly.

I thought about what Sven had said, but here was an opportunity for me to test myself. Just because you have had a successful playing career does not necessarily mean that you can be a good manager. Here was an opportunity to see how I fared. It was a clean sheet of paper and a rare chance to start from scratch and see if I could build a team. I had to weigh that up against the realities of the situation, too. Stockport only had eight players and preseason was imminent, so I would have to find a bunch of decent players very, very quickly and get them up to the high levels of fitness needed just to compete in the Blue Square Conference. On top of that Stockport sold its stadium some years ago to the rugby union team Sale Sharks, so a good portion of its revenue goes on renting the stadium back from the Sharks on match days. The training base is a former farm site that had been converted to a football field.

It was a big risk, but the more I thought about it, the more I felt willing to take it on. I said 'Yes' and we held a press conference on 5 July to announce my appointment. I sat there and smiled and answered a few questions, but I was also thinking, 'Shit, the first game of the season is just over four weeks away and I've only got eight players.'

The first thing I did was to start the search for an assistant manager. I wanted someone who was different from me. The last thing I felt I needed was somebody who agreed with everything I said. I wanted someone with a lot of experience who would challenge me when he felt I needed to be challenged. I made a lot of enquires with contacts in the game and a number of names came up, then I homed in on Willie McStay. Willie is the brother of Paul McStay, who played over 500 games for Celtic. Willie played for Celtic himself, as well as a handful of English clubs before going into coaching. He had managed in Ireland, coached the Celtic youth and reserve teams and had a spell managing in Hungary at Ujpest FC.

I approached Willie, who came on board without hesitation. He is authoritarian and is his own man with his own opinions. He's also spent most of his life developing young players, which is something that will be essential for a club like Stockport County.

I wanted to get an early look at the standard in the Blue Square Conference and thought it would be a good idea to head up to Barrow to take in a preseason friendly. Willie got behind the wheel and I navigated as we journeyed up to Barrow, a place I'd never been to before. I've played all over the world, but reality began to hit home as I realised that when you go on these trips someone has to plan all the logistics to get you to where you are supposed to be and back again. As a player it's all done for you and you don't have to think about it. I had a good grasp of the locations of major cities and towns in England, but not remote places like Barrow. What I was about to find out was that Scots have an even hazier picture of the geography south of Hadrian's Wall than Germans do.

I was quite pleased that I had successfully navigated us to Barrow, but I was surprised at how small the place was. There was a little school, a chip shop and a park in among streets of houses. It looked more of a village than a town. I said to Willie, 'How the hell can this place sustain a Conference team?' After circling several times we couldn't see any signs that said 'Football Ground', so I got out and asked some locals, a man and a woman. 'Where is Barrow Football Club?'

The locals looked at me like I was the village idiot. 'Oooooh, there's no football club here love. Although I think the primary school have a team,' said the woman.

I was confused by this but persisted saying, 'Yes there is. Barrow FC, they are in the Blue Square Conference.'

The man nodded slowly. 'Aye. That's right. That'll be Barrow-in Furness. This is Barrow, Lancashire. You need to keep going north for about eighty miles.'

I gave him an embarrassed 'thank you' and made a face like I was a confused German tourist. I'd made my first managerial cock-up but at least it wasn't on the pitch. We managed to get up to Barrow-*in-Furness* in time to see the game and assess the standard. Coincidentally, shortly afterwards we signed a former Barrow player who became our first signing. Funnily enough he was a Scouser.

We kept our feelers out and ran a series of trial games. Gradually we began to sign up players who we felt could make the grade. Having signed a Scouser, we then followed this with another Scouser, a Scouser, another Scouser and then a Scouser. With Liverpool-based owners, a former Liverpool player as manager and the first five players in all Scousers, inevitably we were dubbed Scouseport County.

While we were on the player hunt, Tony Evans got into a new technology tangle that I didn't quite understand because

I don't do social networking and I don't really understand any of the details of Twitter. We'd had a couple of trialists and Tony innocently tweeted his followers to ask which of the two players they preferred. The press seemed to pick this up as if it was an X Factor-type game show and suggested that I was going to sign whichever player the fans voted for.

When I heard about this I wasn't happy and told Tony that this was not the way I intended to do things, and that I would make the decisions on who signs for the club and nobody else. Tony was very apologetic and said that the press had picked up on his tweet and misconstrued it. I accepted that, but we didn't sign either of the players concerned and Willie and I went about the process of adding to the squad using the old-fashioned tried and tested methods. We watched, we assessed, we took out references and we trialled, being careful not to act too hastily even though with the season fast approaching time was not on our side.

I'm a big believer that you build a football club by winning football matches and that it's best to steer clear of gimmicks like Twitter. It may have its uses and its value, but I don't rate it when it comes to building football teams. Also I think that speculating about other clubs' players is disrespectful, even on Twitter, and I wouldn't be happy if people started doing it to us. I think it also sends out the wrong messages to players that they can say and tweet what they want. I was trying to create a close, tight-knit group, and that meant that when we had gripes and problems we would deal with them in-house and not in the media, whether it was social media or otherwise.

In addition to the players that Willie and I were hunting, agents were continuously on the phone to me. I don't mind that, they have a job to do and often they can be useful in bringing opportunities to your attention. What I dislike is when agents start to do things that are not in the long-term interests of either the player or the club. It reminds me of a story that was told to me by a friend who was the lawyer that represented Michael Ballack when he moved to Chelsea. The deal was done and Michael went out to Sardinia to do preseason training with the Chelsea squad. The lawyer followed and arranged to meet Jose Mourinho for a chat. They met at a rooftop restaurant and Mourinho was relaxed and ordered himself a gin and tonic. It was all very pleasant and Michael's representative asked Mourinho, 'How are things with Michael?'

Mourinho had the air of a man on holiday and replied, 'Very good. Michael is exactly what I expected. Exactly what I wanted.' The representative was not given a moment to suggest what he may have wanted to meet to discuss before Mourinho switched from holiday mode to that 'Special One' glare and said, 'But I tell you something. If he fuck with me. I fuck him first.'

Obviously you have to look after the well-being of your people, but if something starts to disrupt or stand in the way of the progress of the football club, you have to show a bit of steel. Even in those first few weeks at Stockport County I had occasions when agents were badly advising some players and I had to make my position clear.

So we had a lot going on in the background, and just two short weeks into my managerial career we had our first preseason friendly away to New Mills of the Evo-Stik League. This was a big thing for New Mills. In its 125-year history it had never gone higher than the Evo-Stik League. Stockport was the nearest professional team – this was their local derby. It was a compact stadium with a capacity of 1,400 people; 800 turned up that night. I was just about able to field a team and fill the bench with the players that we had cobbled together and added to the existing contingent. We had hardly had time to get fit let alone begin to gel as a team. As I looked out and we were struggling against New Mills of the Evo-Stik League I began to think to myself, 'What the hell have I done? What am I doing here?' We struggled to get a 1–1 draw against a team some fifty league places below us. Yet this is what I wanted. I wanted the opportunity to test myself as a manager. Hey, and what did I have to complain about? I had the luxury of four whole weeks to find nine or ten players, get them fit and gel them into a team before our first match at Forest Green.

We continued to trial potential new players and seek out lads with proven experience. We got them fit using a little of the old and a little of the new. One day we had them pulling weights across the car park like players did in the sixties. Another day they were doing Bikram yoga – that's a 90-minute session involving 26 postures in a room heated to 105 degrees Fahrenheit and at 40 per cent humidity. You can't do that every week if you're in full training, but it's a good addition to the overall programme and it brought a bit of variety to preseason.

Next we had to sort out the diet. When I first arrived they were having sandwiches and curry for lunch after training. I brought someone in to make sure that they were being given healthy and nutritious options. Then we tackled the training ground. Being an old farm it's got a barn, so I got some decorators in and we turned it into a small accommodation block for some of the lads that we brought in. We got the grass properly cut and hedges trimmed. We might not have had the best of facilities, but there was absolutely no reason why we couldn't make them look as professional as possible. I wanted to create a climate of professionalism in everything that we did and how we approached things.

After my early doubts on the touchline at New Mills I was beginning to find the whole experience totally absorbing. It was a breath of fresh air for me and it felt like a new lease of life. There were so many things to think about, snap decisions to be made and my phone never seemed to stop ringing. I hadn't quite started moving the salt and pepper pots at the dinner table, but I was thinking about the job every waking moment and relishing every minute of it.

By the time we went to Buxton for another preseason game we were starting to look like a team and got a 2–0 win. With the sparse crowd of a few hundred the last thing you would have expected was any trouble, but the police helicopter had to be scrambled due to a small handful of fans causing trouble in the peaceful spa town that is Buxton. Apparently a small group of people have been banned from County's home games, so they tend to try to follow the team to away games. As a result a number of our away fixtures are being switched to Fridays to make it harder for this group to travel and infiltrate. Unfortunately it affects our genuine fans in equal measure.

There was some comfort for the fans. The new consortium were keen to boost the home attendances and came up with a scheme that they wanted to run for our first Saturday home game. GT Law, which as well as leading the consortium was the shirt sponsor, specialises in personal-injury law. For the layman that means that if you have an accident they represent you on a 'no-win, no-fee' basis. Tony Evans had an idea. He wanted to do a 'no-win, no-fee' offer for the fans. Newcomers to the division, Ebbsfleet, were down on the fixture list as our first Saturday home game. The Stockport Board offered to repay the fans' entry fee if we lost against Ebbsfleet, provided that fans bought their tickets in advance. This applied to both home and away fans. Technically it was a 'no-win-or-draw, no fee' basis because we had to lose for the refund to be applicable. It was a pretty big risk because the financial loss would be in the region of £40,000 if we lost the game.

In our first game of the season I think that we must have broken some form of league record, because ten players in the starting line-up were making their debuts. Only the goalkeeper had played for Stockport County before. Then I brought on three substitutes who were also debutants, so that made thirteen. I find it hard to imagine that anyone has ever done that before. After an away draw at Forest Green and a home win to Kettering, we now had a chance to assess ourselves at this level. We were bringing a lot of players together very quickly and it was impossible to know if we had made the right decisions and begun to get them into the right sort of shape for this league. But our early encounters were promising and I knew that we could improve, so we went into the Ebbsfleet game with a positive outlook. I made sure that the players didn't think about the 'no-win, no fee' scheme. I mentioned it once and told them to put it out of their minds. Our job was always the same, regardless of what was going on off the pitch: we were interested only in winning.

We played well against Ebbsfleet and made a hatful of chances that we should have taken and finished them off. Our pressure eventually told and we took the lead after sixty-nine minutes. Five minutes later, I learnt something that I could only learn by doing what I am doing – jumping in at the deep end and learning to be a manager. I got into a form of substitute hokey-cokey with the referee. I wanted to make a change and I told the fourth official.

The referee said, 'No you can't bring him on yet, hold him there.'

I said, 'No, I want him on now.'

The substitute was walking backwards and forwards as the argument went on between me, the fourth official and the referee. Meanwhile Ebbsfleet took a throw, it was headed on and driven into our net to make it 1–1. I had confused and distracted the players, who were watching the substitute shenanigans. I was mad at myself because I think I contributed to that goal even though I was on the touchline. I could have bluffed it and carried on as though it was nothing to do with me, but that is not the style of management that I want. I'm as accountable as everyone else and as soon as the game was over I called the players together in the dressing room. I held my hands in the air and said, 'Lads, I hold my hands up. I have to take my share of the blame for their goal. I made a mistake and I'm sorry.' I think that it is important that they see that I will stand up and be counted.

The game ended 1–1. Tony Evans would have liked a win,

but he was relieved that we had got a draw and he had no need to pay out the £40,000 that his 'no-win, no fee' scheme would have cost him if we lost. When Willie McStay and I sat down after the game we were very disappointed to have got a draw. Later as the fog lifted a bit, I realised something. Just four weeks earlier we could barely field a team and were relieved to scrape a draw at lowly New Mills. Now we were extremely disappointed because we drew against a Blue Square Conference side. To me this meant that we had made a lot of progress in just four short weeks. It was quite a journey and an intense and exhilarating time in my life.

In between our first couple of games, something happened that deeply disturbed me and was one of the few things that took my mind away from eating, drinking and sleeping Stockport County. I love England and I don't think that's because I wear rose-tinted spectacles and have a tourist's view of the country. Don't forget I've seen Liverpool warts and all under the guidance of the Cultural Attaché for Bootle. I know that there are problems in the country, but I was completely taken aback by the riots that took place in August 2011. I could have just watched it on television and then got on with my work, but I felt so strongly about what I was seeing I couldn't forget about it.

This is a moment of truth for England. Something has happened to this country that is damaging the very fabric of all that made it great. I don't believe that those riots were about poverty or race. People were not coming out of shops with loaves of bread and baskets of fish. They were loaded up with giant plasma TVs, expensive trainers and mobile phones. Those are not the actions of a hungry minority of people, those are the actions of wolves that will devour and destroy anything that is vulnerable. This is said to be a problem in English society. I would disagree. The problem is that the benefits system, which was a marvellous innovation designed to protect those most in need, has developed in such a way as to create a pack of people who sit outside of society. That's not the same as saying that everyone in receipt of benefits is part of this culture. This is another damaging thing. Decent, respectable people sometimes need the help of the state yet they can easily get stigmatised as if they are a part of this group that feeds off the system, putting nothing back into society. It's wrong that good people get tarnished in this way.

Already I can feel the emerging backlash against such comments, but therein lies another problem. Anyone who is prepared to say it as it is gets treated as if they are a Holocaust denier, a racist or a fascist. Proper debate of this problem is stifled by politicians who are more interested in buying votes than facing up to reality, and are fearful of associating with anything that may cause offence to anyone. This country must face up to reality very, very quickly or face the equivalent of a new kind of Viking invasion, this time from within its own shores. Something bad has taken hold on the edges of society and soundbites, slogans and gimmicks will not cure it.

This will take a generation to deal with, but only if the country sets out on a course of consistently building structure and discipline right across society, including within the enclaves that regard themselves as outside of society. Some people won't like it, some will fall by the wayside and some who fail to conform may get hurt. But pain is a great teacher. Right now, it seems that you can wreak havoc in this country without any serious consequences.

So many of those involved in the riots are said to have no male role model in their lives. That's not a valid excuse. And why is it that the state supports and in some cases incentivises people to have children who will grow up in a situation where there is little probability of any structure or social norms being imposed on the children? This liberal approach of so-called equity and fairness is all very laudable and can be rationalised on paper beautifully by those who went to Eton, Oxford and Cambridge, but they are not the people that have to live with the fallout of this phenomenon that they continue to feed. In any case, where is the fairness in perpetuating families that are third-generation unemployed? Where is the fairness and equity in that?

I don't like what is happening to this country. We can stand back and blame this politician or that politician or we can try to do something. I've got my hands more than full at the moment, but I am determined that I must do something, even if at this stage it is just a small thing that I can build on in the future. I'm lending my support to an organisation I came across through my Liverpool connection. Silver Track Training provides opportunities for young people from troubled backgrounds by training them for jobs in the railway industry and fast-tracking them into employment through the apprenticeship route. They can demonstrate real success in doing this and the stories of some of the young people who have managed to turn their lives around are truly inspiring. I think that we all have to do whatever we can to support those who can create structure and purpose for those who really need it if they are to contribute to our society. I know only too well what can happen when the scaffolding of your life starts to wobble. That's made me even more determined to do what little I can to help others, particularly young people, to build their own scaffolding.

Tony Evans had joined the Stockport County board and was clearly having a major influence over the running of the club. I joined on the basis of the discussions that we had with each other before the season started and the promises that were made to me, particularly around budgets and the ability to build a squad from practically nothing.

I just got on with my work. There was no time to lose because we needed to be able to field some sort of a team on the opening day of the season. That was my priority.

The takeover was not finalised, but it felt like it was simply a matter of time. Everybody believed that the takeover was going through and we all carried on in that belief.

By the middle of September, we were lying 16th in the table. For a team assembled from scratch we had done quite well, but our inability to hold on to a lead had seen us clocking up draw after draw after draw. The league table doesn't lie and our position was where we deserved to be. There was still time to consolidate. Based on Tony's promises, the squad could be improved and I expected that we would make some steady if not world shattering progress during the course of the season.

Word started to leak out that there were problems with the takeover, which before had seemed like it was pretty much a done deal. A liability of £200,000 had been identified during the due diligence process and this had become a continued matter of debate between the consortium and the existing board.

I have no idea whose interpretation of the responsibility for that liability was the correct one. It seemed that the consortium felt that the existing board should pick up that tab, whilst the existing board thought the opposite. There was a stalemate and the consortium pulled out, leaving the club without the investment that it was expecting.

We carried on, because there was nothing that we could do to affect this situation off the pitch. On the pitch, we were continuing to frustrate both ourselves and our fans. We were developing a habit of conceding very late goals and dropping valuable points. We began to drift into the wrong half of the table.

The realities of the situation were beginning to hit home, as the promises that Tony made to me on the basis of the consortium taking over could not now be delivered. A fresh fan-backed consortium came forward with a proposed fresh manager in Stockport County legend Jim Gannon. That's fine; I have no problems with that.

I did have a problem with the board allowing the consortium

to hold a meeting in the club lounge immediately after a home game, which we drew 3–3 having been in front 3–1 and again conceding with three minutes left.

To have a prospective new manager in your club in any circumstances, but especially when we were scrapping for points, is unacceptable; it felt unprofessional and I saw it as undermining my position. Whether it was a deliberate act or done out of naivety I don't know, but it was something that I just could not ignore.

We were not performing as we should have been and the buck stops here for that, but I have to remind myself that a few months earlier there wasn't even a team to put out on to the pitch. The promises that had been made to me by Tony, which formed the basis of my decision to leave Leicester City, could not and would not be honoured, and I felt that the board were undermining my role.

The only part of this that I had signed up to was being accountable for results and that was not a problem. The broken promises and courting of a new manager were unacceptable to me.

I was enjoying the work as a manager. It was challenging, I was learning a lot, but I could not stay under these circumstances. I felt that my position was untenable and the chairman accepted my resignation. Eight days later Jim Gannon was installed as the new Stockport County manager.

I was disappointed with the way things had turned out, but once I had got over that I was able to confirm something for myself. Football management *is* for me. I know quite clearly that it is what I want to do. Some players have a go and then decide that it is not for them. I've had a go and I know that it *is* for me. It's a shame that my future wasn't at Stockport, but I'll wait for another opportunity and go into it even better prepared, because of what I have learned about management and about myself.

A couple of years ago there was a Radio 4 programme that poked fun at Stockport. The programme's name was a parody of that famous song 'New York, New York (So Good They Named It Twice)'. It was called *Stockport, So Good They Named It Once*, which is very funny, but the implication is that Stockport is not a very nice place. I don't go along with that. Stockport for me will always be a very good place. It's the place where I had a chance to cut my teeth as a manager and a place where I had a chance to learn a few lessons.

I've had a lot to look back on in my life and one of the dearest things to me is that in good times and in bad I'll always be able to return to Anfield and to Liverpool, my spiritual home. Importantly, I feel that I have a lot to look forward to. I continue to be positive, I continue to go forward and I continue to live by the words of one of my great mentors, Sven Goran-Erickson: 'Life, Kaiser. We are celebrating life'.

I continue to celebrate life.

INDEX

Note: DH stands for Dietmar Hamann. Subheadings for individuals are in chronological order. Unless otherwise stated, names of countries, cities or towns refer to teams.